Rock and Roll Revealed

Rock and Roll Revealed

The Outrageous Lives of Rock's Biggest Stars

Maryanne Melloan

Friedman Group

A FRIEDMAN GROUP BOOK

Copyright © 1993 by Michael Friedman Publishing Group, Inc.

ISBN 0-8317-5159-2

ROCK AND ROLL REVEALED
The Outrageous Lives of Rock's Biggest Stars
was prepared and produced by
Michael Friedman Publishing Group, Inc.
15 West 26th Street
New York, NY 10010

Editor: Elizabeth Viscott Sullivan
Art Director: Jeff Batzli
Designer: Susan E. Livingston
Photography Editors: Daniella Nilva and Colleen Branigan

Printed in Hong Kong and bound in China by Leefung-Asco Printers Ltd.

Acknowledgments

Deepest gratitude to Miguel Arteta, Mark Drop, Bill Dumas, Johanna Farrand, Neil Krupnick, Terry Kannofsky, Rick Low, Vivi Mata, Tony Maxwell, Mary Petrie-Lowen, Hillary Rollins, Diana Soule, Sean P. Steele, Liz Sullivan, Rich Wilkes, and my wonderful family for all their help.

Contents

Introduction

Rock and roll has never been about good clean fun—and that's exactly why teenagers around the world like it. Even with the moon-in-June lyrics, even with the arrival of Liverpool's cuddly mop-tops, even in the era of flower-child innocence, even in the Osmond Brothers' pearly smiles, rock and roll has always been a sweaty, sexy, nasty business.

The very first bona fide rock and roll song (by most accounts), Bill Haley's "Rock Around the Clock," was the theme of *Blackboard Jungle*, a film about teen gang violence—no wonder the Establishment feared the power of rock and roll. Conservatives dubbed its raucous sounds "the Devil's music" and tried to shield their impressionable offspring from its negative influence. One early fan's characterization of Elvis Presley—"He's just one big hunk of forbidden fruit"— aptly describes the allure of rock and roll at the time—and today.

In the fifties, rock music was new, naughty, and best of all, accessible: any schmuck could pick out three chords on a guitar. And, amazingly to the pimply high school misfit, those three chords could land you fame, fortune, and homecoming queens in droves. As Don Henley said about his early pursuit of rock and roll fame, "Money and girls were the two big motivations—that's what it was for everybody."

When the three-chord fifties evolved into the Dylan-and-Beatles sixties, rock and roll became a vehicle for trying to change the world—or at least, an excuse for using drugs to rearrange the chemical balance of one's brain. And rock stars led the way, with "mind-expanding" lyrics and conspicuous consumption of anything that could be smoked, swallowed, or sniffed. By the seventies and eighties, rock musicians were glorified paragons of excess, adolescent millionaires who fed their fans' fantasies by publicly indulging their hungry ids. As Vince Neil of Mötley Crüe said about the rock and roll life, "I think if you take sex, drugs, and rock and roll, let your imagination run wild, and then multiply it by ten, then you'll have an idea of what our life has been like."

Sounds like quite a party, but one you'd definitely regret having attended the next morning. Nevertheless, the great rock and roll Babylon is strewn with casualties, talented musicians who always wanted to push everything just one step further. As sphinxlike Keith Richards said, "Obviously, there was drugs in rock and roll, and the sex wasn't too bad. But I don't know anybody that actually lives like that all the time. I used to know a few guys that did that, but they're not alive anymore, you know? And you get the message after you've been to a few funerals."

Drugs and sex are not the only areas in which rock stars are larger than life. In their homes, spending habits, practical jokes, marriages, and fashion choices, rockers' tastes run to the excessive and extravagant. A house with a 10,000-square-foot (900 sq m) interior was a little small for Cher, there was always a more desirable blonde model in the wings for Rod Stewart, Madonna has had to make her image more shocking with each new venture, and so on.

Understandably, many rock stars grew up in modest circumstances and can't get enough goodies out of the cookie jar once they've got it in their grasp. And certainly, inventive flamboyance helps distinguish performers in a crowded field. But insatiability of any kind can lead to early burnout.

The question is: are the music and the Caligula life-style inseparable? Can rock musicians satisfy their adoring fans without—to paraphrase the Doors—their mutual love becoming a funeral pyre? Maybe. But what fun would that be?

Chapter One

On the Road
Again

TOURING

But as a band's bottom line swells, touring gets considerably more cushy. After a couple of hit albums in the early seventies, Led Zeppelin was awarded a converted Boeing 720B jet dubbed the *Starship,* complete with a long bar, overstuffed seats, video screens, bedrooms with fake fireplaces, showers, and an organ. Jimmy Page was extremely afraid of flying, but the plush *Starship* and liberal libations softened the edges. Suddenly, getting from gig to gig was not such a grind: "It was a f--- ing flying gin palace!" says tour manager Richard Cole.

Clearly, this was not just another jumbo jet, and indeed, the role of stewardess was no easy task. One young woman had to be saved from an amorous attack by Zep drummer John "Bonzo the Beast" Bonham; smooth-talking Page was recruited to soothe the screaming girl's nerves.

When successful bands reach their destinations and check into hotels, the pampering continues. If rock stars are treated like children, it's because they often are just out of their teens and completely unaccustomed to the world of chic accommodations. As Elton John told *Rolling Stone* in 1992: "My whole life I'd never lived on my own.... I was on tour with people constantly around me. In the morning I'd get up, wash, get ready for the day, and from then on there were dozens of people to do everything for me." After his divorce from recording engineer Renate Blauel in 1988, John was finally on his own. "For months, I stayed in my bedroom, too scared to go out, just doing the *Times* crossword puzzle. When I got up the courage to travel, I'd phone all my friends, incredibly excited. 'Hey, do you know what?' I'd say, 'I checked into this hotel all by myself!'"

If John was a pampered child on tour, Zeppelin's Bonzo was an enfant terrible. Publicist Danny Goldberg notes that "Bonzo was a huge adult with the emotions of a six-year-old child, and an artistic license to indulge in any sort of

No more rubbing shoulders with mere mortals at airports: Led Zeppelin's forty-seat Starship *transported the band in style and privacy.*

Los Angeles, 1973. An angry resident complains to management of the Hyatt House that some members of Led Zeppelin are dumping their drinks on his parked car from their eleventh-floor window. A manager is doing his best to calm him when suddenly...crash! The man's Lincoln Town Car is all but demolished by a plummeting table. So much for the drinks.

What is it about touring with a rock band that turns one's thoughts to mayhem? Is it the boredom, the exhaustion, the drugs, or the music itself that brings out the Devil in the ordinary guitar-playing Joe?

In the early days, tours were often badly planned, which meant that the band and crew were faced with an overwhelming schedule. Susie Wynne Wilson, a friend of Pink Floyd in the late sixties, remembers steering the tour bus for the bone-weary driver while he slept—at the wheel—with his foot jammed against the accelerator. Unlicensed Susie steered the troupe around Great Britain, occasionally waking the driver to alert him to impending peril. "Imagine what it was like," she laughs, "waking from a deep sleep to find yourself in the driver's seat rapidly approaching some disaster."

infantile or destructive behavior that amused him." Most hotel managers were not so amused. The Tokyo Hilton closed its doors to Led Zeppelin after Bonzo and Cole had a contest to see how much havoc they could wreak on their rooms with a pair of newly purchased samurai swords.

At one hotel, Zeppelin was given an entire floor. Cole roamed from one end to the other on his Honda, steering past the legions of barely teenage female fans who slept outside Jimmy Page's door. And wherever Zeppelin stayed, it was always raining furniture; the band particularly enjoyed watching large color televisions explode upon hitting the ground. On one particular occasion, the band treated a party-minded hotel manager to a television hurling. Zep manager Peter Grant bellowed his approval—"Have one on us!"—supervised the ejection, and handed the manager $500.

Another Zeppelin tour anecdote involves their comparatively reserved bassist, John Paul Jones. One night, after a drunken Zep rampage through New Orleans, Jones took a conquest back to his hotel. The two apparently smoked a joint and then passed out drunk, accidentally igniting the sheets. Jones and his companion were soon awakened by firemen who steered them out of the burning room. Jones was startled, but he was even more shocked to see his almost-lover half-dressed, and that "she" possessed decidedly male anatomy. Jones had mistakenly picked up a transvestite and took no small amount of ribbing for his error from his fellow band members.

The Rolling Stones were also involved in accidental hotel arson, resulting from candles supplied by a New York hotel during the blackout of 1965. The band was having a typical party: plenty of booze, plenty of drugs, and plenty of young women gradually doffing their clothing. Indeed, everyone there was in such high spirits that it took a moment or two before people

realized that a burning bed was not part of the makeshift lighting plan. The girls became the designated firemen, battling the flames with water from ice buckets. The fire was subdued, and the lights came back on to reveal a half-naked, sooty ensemble in various sordid stages of lovemaking.

Rounding out the boisterous supergroup triumvirate of the sixties and seventies was none other than that expert demolition team, the Who. Bonzo's drummer double in the Who, Keith Moon, rivaled his colleagues in imaginative hotel carnage. Moon's legendary exploits include nailing an entire suite of furniture to a hotel-room ceiling, using firecrackers to blow up toilets, and driving a Lincoln Continental into the pool

at a Holiday Inn. On one occasion in Los Angeles, Moon dropped several boxes of detergent into a fountain from a twelfth-story hotel room. The bubbles foamed out of the fountain and frothed down the street. From above, Moon sipped one-hundred-year-old cognac and admired his handiwork.

Occasionally, rockers cause hotel hysteria without meaning to. Alice Cooper tells a hotel story about his pet boa constrictor, Veronica, a creature measuring fifteen feet (4.5m) that Cooper would sometimes use as a stage prop. One day Cooper left the snake relaxing in the bathroom of his suite at the Knoxville, Tennessee, Marriott. When he returned, the snake had escaped down the toilet. Cooper notified

Why rock stars should have private jets: Rod Stewart and entourage make their mark on a British Airways first-class cabin in 1977.

McKagan once beat up the drummer of Faster Pussycat, bound him with duct tape, and dumped him in an elevator.

Even the likes of squeaky-clean New Kid on the Block Donnie Wahlberg can get crazy. In 1991, the youngster allegedly baptized a Louisville, Kentucky, hallway with vodka, tossed a lighted match, and sat down to enjoy the blaze. Little damage was done, but the hotel pressed charges. Wahlberg's lawyers had to work overtime to beat a first-degree arson rap.

And the pranks don't stop at the stage door. Touring entourages often lighten the pressure with silly practical jokes at gig time. Once, Steve Winwood's crew hired a woman to walk onstage during a set, open her trench coat, and flash the band. Old pro that he is, Steve kept right on playing.

On another occasion, Mick Fleetwood and John McVie took advantage of Eagle Don Henley's interest in Stevie Nicks. Henley and Nicks hadn't yet met, but he had called her once or twice by

Above: Alice Cooper with slippery pal, Veronica. Right: Why New Kids shouldn't play with matches: Donnie Wahlberg faces arson charges in Kentucky.

the manager, but the snake could not be found. Two weeks later, Cooper read a blurb in the paper about singer Charlie Pride walking into his hotel bathroom and seeing an enormous snake coming out of the toilet.

Touring madness was not just a by-product of the freewheeling hippie era: plenty of televisions still sail out hotel windows today. The capers of metallic wonders Guns N' Roses tend to run to the violent. Axl Rose once beat up a businessman in a hotel bar for saying the singer looked like Jon Bon Jovi; guitarist Izzy Stradlin and bassist Duff

Rock and Roll REVEALED

the time the two bands shared a bill. When Stevie entered her dressing room that night she found a huge bouquet of roses and a card that read, "The best of my love…Tonight? Love, Don." Christine McVie took a furious Stevie aside after a few minutes and pointed out the authors of the note, Fleetwood and McVie, giggling in a corner. Says Fleetwood, "It was awhile before Stevie felt like talking to either of us again."

Not all release valves are as harmless as these, however. One night after a gig in Amsterdam, a drunk Mick Jagger and Keith Richards staggered back to their hotel. From Richards' room, Jagger phoned upstairs to Charlie Watts, waking him up. "Is that my drummer? Why don't you get your arse down here?" Watts got dressed, came to Richards' room, and proceeded to plant a rather swift right hook on Jagger's jaw, squarely knocking the stunned singer into a plateful of smoked salmon. According to Richards, Jagger "almost floated out the window along the table into a canal. I just grabbed his leg and saved him from going out." Charlie berated Jagger: "Don't you ever call me 'your drummer' again. You're *my* f--- ing singer!"

Of course, many bands let off steam on the road with plain old Jack Daniel's-and-groupies, rock-and-roll partying. *Rolling Stone* journalist Mikal Gilmore describes a typical backstage scene with Van Halen in the early days: "As ZZ Top's 'I'm Bad, I'm Nationwide' pours out of [David Lee] Roth's portable stereo, two young women climb up on the banquet table and cheerfully strip down to their boots and panties, to the rowdy delight of the men and the silence of the other women…. Alex [Van Halen] thoughtfully produces a flashlight, which he uses to illuminate the dancers' pelvic motions. In return, the women…rub themselves…. Roth comes over and gives me a fraternal slap on the shoulder. 'Lost denizens of the night,' he says, smiling at the women writhing on the table. 'Man, I relate to them heavily.'"

But even the bad boys of rock and roll eventually get tired of wild life on the road. Surprisingly, even Led Zeppelin was sick of the debauchery by the mid-seventies, and secretly worried about how they looked in photographs and whether their wives would be mad at them for behaving badly. (The wives were particularly skeptical of the band's Los Angeles visits; the city was notorious for its "anything goes" milieu and eager underage groupies. Band members sometimes asked their tour director to draw up phony tour itineraries for their wives, substituting supposedly less marriage-threatening cities for Los Angeles engagements.)

Sting has one possible answer for why rock and roll musicians thrive on lives of mayhem: "I tried drugs, I tried screwing every woman who came into the room—all that stuff….I've often manufactured crisis to feel alive or creative. There's nothing worse than everything going well."

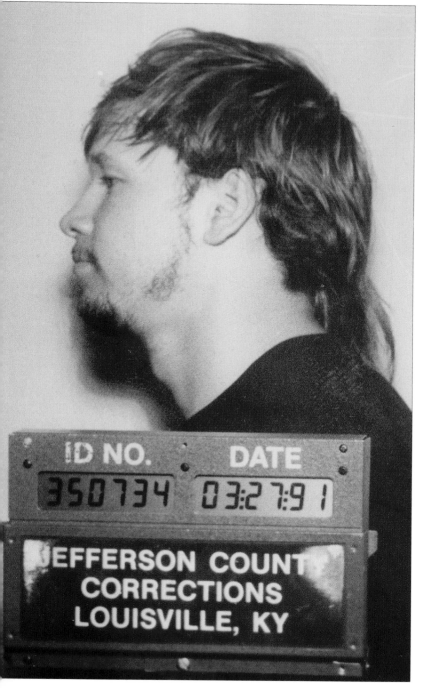

15

Ziggy Played Guitar

PERFORMING

Above: *James Brown's electrifying stage act inspired performers from Michael Jackson to George Michael. Right: The riff that launched a thousand careers: Chuck Berry's signature licks and showmanship are the guitarist's template.*

The amazing thing about the great rock and roll bands is that no matter how much energy is expended defenestrating furniture, obliging young girls, and soaring to new heights of intoxication, they always have some left over to enflame the clubs and arenas of the world with their thrilling musical pyrotechnics.

Each performer has his or her own way of manipulating the audience. As Lemmy of Motorhead says, "An audience is like an animal; sometimes you have to tickle it under the chin, but sometimes you have to slap it around the muzzle to get its attention."

One of the great muzzle-slappers of all time has to be James Brown. Never one for subtlety, the Godfather of Soul used to "shoot out of the wings like a pinball off the spring with a 'pleeeeese!' that could pop a hairpin at fifty feet [15m]," according to Gerri Hirshey of *Rolling Stone*. Rock writer Robert Palmer elaborates: "He does a split, erupts into a pirouette, whirls like a dervish, and ends up at the microphone just in time to shriek 'Bayba-a-ay' as the band modulates into the introduction to his latest hit." And all this in costumes such as an all-crimson number with the large word "SEX" blaring from the waistband.

In later years, Brown's stage persona was occasionally dissipated by his drug of choice, marijuana spiked with angel dust. In the middle of his hellfire histrionics, Brown would stop the band midsong, stare into space, and start murmuring non sequiturs. But when he was at his best, as Bill Wyman once put it, "You could put Jerry Lee Lewis, Little Richard, Chuck Berry, and Bo Diddley on one side of the stage and James Brown on the other, and you wouldn't even notice the others were up there!"

Actually, Wyman's is an apples-and-oranges comparison; each rock great named has had his own distinctive brand of hypertheatrics. Lewis and Little Richard both pounded pianos into sawdust as they howled their raunchy lyrics, Lewis occasionally setting his instrument on fire. Chuck Berry's famous duck-walk maneuver may seem tame compared to the gymnastics of a David Lee Roth, but—combined with Berry's 1,000-watt showmanship—it never fails to bring down the house. And Bo Diddley, well, the signature "thunk-a-thunk-a-thunk, a-thunk-thunk" beat is enough to set fans screaming.

Wyman's own former band has never been in short supply of kinetic energy, thanks primarily to frontman dervish Mick Jagger. In A.E. Hotchner's book on the Stones, *Blown Away*, Jagger's ex-girlfriend Marianne Faithfull

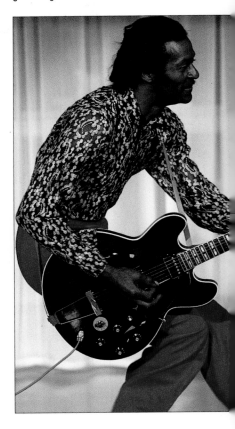

Rock and Roll REVEALED

claims that Jagger derived his stage persona from watching Tina Turner perform: "...he would practice what he had seen in front of the mirror, endlessly dancing, gesturing, watching himself, moving his body rhythmically, the way Tina did."

But Jagger made Turner's great moves his own, and he eventually blossomed into one of the most mesmerizing performers in rock and roll. According to Faithfull, Jagger's entire personality would transform when he was onstage. One night, just after a performance, "He was like somebody possessed. I don't think he even knew who I was. He still had his makeup on, and there was a froth of spittle around his lips. His eyes were violent. He was making sounds, guttural sounds, and he was completely unintelligible.... He picked me up and slammed me against

the wall. Several times. He was like a mad creature from some hostile planet. Not the human race."

Whatever demons Jagger conjured up, the audience responded. In the sixties, several Stones concerts were stopped due to crowd hysteria. Stage-front bouncers resorted to punching and karate-chopping crazed girls trying to get to the band. On one occasion in Montreal, police "quieted" fans by ramming their heads into a wooden fence. The Stones had to pick their way through the detritus of fifty prone bodies on their way offstage.

At a Blackpool, England, concert in 1964, journalist Roy Carr remembers seeing Keith Richards discourage a fan from climbing onstage with a boot to the face. Fans were so wild they managed to pull a Steinway grand piano off the stage. After the show, keyboardist

Ian Stewart brought the band wood-splinter remnants of their guitars and amps as souvenirs. And this is all when shows go as planned.

When the show goes awry, the results can be just as dramatic. Keith Richards once brushed a microphone with his metal-inlaid guitar neck and was shocked into unconsciousness for seven minutes.

Another equipment snafu resulted in defining the Who's stage show. During one early gig, Pete Townshend accidentally broke his guitar when the band was playing in a club with a very low ceiling; one upward flourish and the neck snapped. Townshend immediately lost his cool and proceeded to smash the instrument to pieces. Manager Kit Lambert observed the audience's delight and made equipment destruction a Who concert signature. Townshend, however,

Mirror image: Mick's stage act is based on Tina's moves.

hastens to note that—unlike acts like the Sex Pistols or Billy Idol—the Who's smash-ups were not just for show. "When I smashed guitars," says Townshend, "I f---ing well meant it."

Drug and alcohol abuse, of course, have sent many well-planned shows into Never-Never Land. The Doors' front man, Jim Morrison, was a magnetic showman, punctuating his band's hypnotic ragas with howls, snarls, and frenetic stimulant-inspired dancing. He believed he knew how to "diagnose a crowd psychologically"; he could make fans scream, dance, riot, or just stare, trancelike. Occasionally he'd tease the crowd by bringing a song to a dead halt; he'd stand stock-still, silent, sometimes for a minute or two, just to milk the audience's discomfort. "I like to see

how long they can stand it," Morrison said, "and just when they're about to crack, I let 'em go…they get frightened, and fear is very exciting…it's like the moment before you have an orgasm. Everybody wants that. It's a peaking experience."

No wonder critic Ellen Sander nicknamed Morrison "Mickey Mouse de Sade." Morrison preferred to think of himself as an "erotic politician."

Everything Morrison did, he did to the limit. He rarely went onstage without having altered his consciousness in some way, primarily with alcohol. Under the spotlights he found a release for his manic energy and need for self-expression. As he himself put it: "The only time I really open up is onstage. The

mask of performing gives it to me, a place where I can hide myself, then I can reveal myself."

One night, during a Miami concert, he revealed a bit too much of himself. He arrived late to the gig, soused on airplane liquor. Halfway through the second song he stopped singing, and slurred to the audience: "I'm lonely. I need some love, y'all…. Ain't nobody gonna love my a--? Come on." When he failed to elicit the response he wanted, his mood turned foul. He began swearing and berating the audience as "slaves." With a roar of, "I'm not gonna take this s--t!" He began to unbuckle his belt. Keyboardist Ray Manzarek yelled to a roadie to stop him. Morrison had stripped down to boxer

Rock and Roll REVEALED

shorts, but opinions differ on whether or not the singer actually exposed himself. It is noteworthy that he was not arrested on the.spot; charges of lewd behavior, public drunkenness, profanity, and public exposure were levied some three days later.

Miami officials were incensed; there would be no rock star exemptions granted in this case. The trial was a publicity circus. Even the prosecutor was star-struck: as Morrison was leaving the courtroom one day, a young attorney asked him if he might have a copy of the new Doors album, *Absolutely Live*, to spare, as the local record shops had run out of it.

When questioned on the witness stand about whether or not he had exposed himself, Jim accidentally confessed to another of the charges by blurting, "I don't remember. I was too drunk." Oddly, he was acquitted of the drunkenness charge and convicted only of the profanity and exposure charges. The Lizard King was sentenced to six months in jail; the case was still under appeal when he died.

Jimi Hendrix developed his wild stage show early on in his career, while playing behind acts such as Little Richard and the Isley Brothers. Jimi was known for stealing focus from the star performers, with his trailing ribbons and scarves, earring, and outsize Afro. In one delirious blur he'd turn a somersault, pick out a solo with his teeth, drop into a split, and then finish the solo with the guitar behind his back. As biographer David Henderson notes, Jimi "acted as if he were somewhere else, onstage by himself, as if he were the star, instead of just another guitar player begging to sit in."

Of course, it wasn't long before Hendrix became a star attraction. Backstage at a 1967 gig in England, Hendrix knew that he was up against some stiff competition. The teenyboppers had come to see the teen idol acts on the bill—Cat Stevens, Engelbert Humperdinck, the Walker Brothers—

EXPRESS YOURSELF

Memorable Stage Acts

Alice Cooper: Staged mock executions, chopped up baby dolls, wore a live boa constrictor.

Screamin' Jay Hawkins: Had himself wheeled onstage in a flaming coffin.

Janet Jackson: One tour featured a unique stage prop: Janet's pet panther, Rhythm. On one occasion, Rhythm relieved himself onstage. Janet slipped on the slick floor but got up and finished the song, her stage costume adorned with panther pee.

Mötley Crüe: Have been known to chainsaw the heads off mannequins. Also lit themselves on fire.

Ozzy Osbourne: Once bit the head off a bat.

Plasmatics: Lead singer Wendy O. Williams smashed television sets with a sledgehammer, blew up Cadillac Coupe de Villes, and cut guitars in half with a chainsaw.

Iggy Pop: Screamed and wailed, rubbed peanut butter and raw steaks over his body, sliced himself with broken glass, dived into the audience.

Judas Priest: Vocalist Rob Halford used to roar onstage on a Harley.

Prince: Slid down a fire pole, stripped to bikini briefs, then crossed to a brass bed and simulated you-know-what while moaning: "We are now making our final approach to satisfaction. Please bring your lips, your arms, your hips into the up and locked position—for landing!"

Public Image, Ltd: Once performed an entire show behind a scrim. New York fans expressed their disapproval with bellowed epithets and flying beer bottles.

Guitar great Jimi Hendrix had perfect pitch.

fought in my life—inside, you know? And like that wasn't the place to do it, so I just unmasked appearances."

Other bands in the sixties and seventies wowed their chemically adjusted audiences with trippy stage props and sets. Pink Floyd were pioneers of psychedelic rock stage shows. Their sixties concerts were must-sees for the British in-crowd. Early effects involved slithering colored liquids on slides, projected behind the band. From there, they moved on to oddball props; in one

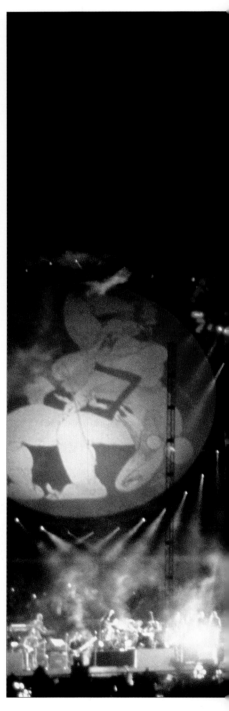

and Hendrix knew he'd have to come up with something special to get their attention. He and his manager came up with the idea of incinerating his guitar during the song "Fire," and quickly dispatched a roadie to pick up some lighter fluid. At the end of the song, Hendrix doused his Stratocaster and lit a match. The flames shot twelve feet (3.6m) high. The crowd went nuts—they'd never seen anything like it before.

Hendrix couldn't burn his guitar every night, so he started to get wilder with it, machine-gunning it from his crotch, humping it as it fed back. As the new act developed, he would let out orgasmic screams in concert with his howling, phallic instrument. There were complaints that the act was too erotic, but Jimi Hendrix Experience tickets were

selling like hotcakes, and the almighty dollar prevailed. Hendrix commented on the complaints: "I play and move as I feel. It's no act. Perhaps it's sexy...but what music with a big beat isn't?"

But years of drug abuse and the greed of managers and hangers-on began to take their toll, and Hendrix's performances suffered. In January 1970, he was headlining at New York's Madison Square Garden for a Vietnam Moratorium Committee benefit. He had taken some bad acid, and it was torturing him. He tried to get through a song, but finally took off his guitar. He told nineteen thousand fans, "I'm sorry, we just can't get it together," and walked offstage. Hendrix noted the irony that the event was a peace rally, "and here I am fighting the biggest war I've ever

Rock and Roll REVEALED

1967 concert, Floyd's music was augmented by the percussion of potatoes hurled at a gong and the amplified sound of wood being sawed.

By 1969, the carpentry motif had expanded: the band actually built a table; they sawed and hammered along to taped music. When the pieces were complete, roadies assembled the table and set it for tea. The band then sat down, poured out the tea, and switched on a miked transistor radio to whatever happened to be on the airwaves.

A 1971 outdoor Floyd concert featured a fifty-foot (15m) inflatable octopus rising out of a lake. The fake sea creature was impressive, but all the real fish in the lake floated belly up from the trauma of the music's volume.

But Floyd's "The Wall" tour was the band's most extravagant show. During the course of the concert, roadies systematically erected a thirty-five-foot (10.5m) wall of cardboard bricks, obscuring the band from view. Bassist Roger Waters inserted the last brick himself. Guitarist David Gilmour was then hydraulically hoisted to the top of the Wall for his "Comfortably Numb" solo. For the concert's finale, the Wall exploded back into a pile of bricks. Quite a coup for the design team.

The punk movement of the seventies heralded a significant change of direction for rock stage acts. Sex Pistol Johnny Rotten's "I Hate Pink Floyd" T-shirt said it all; the punks scoffed at the synth-laden, overblown pretensions of bands like Floyd. The Pistols' sweat-

For a specially arranged concert held in Berlin in 1990, Pink Floyd mastermind Roger Waters organized the construction of an enormous wall and giant puppets of characters from **The Wall.**

and-sneer bombast was a true return to simplicity: gone were the sets and light shows, gone were the backing tapes; indeed, gone was any semblance of musical competence. A Sex Pistols show was strictly about attitude, not music. The frustrated, disaffected youth of England, and then the entire world, embraced Rotten's anarchic rebellion, loving him even as he screamed "I hate you!" from the stage. Self-destructive mayhem replaced self-indulgent solos as Rotten roamed the stage, stabbing out lit cigarettes on his arms and

scratching his face with needles. This was truly a wake-up call for the stoner audiences of the acid-rock era.

Meanwhile, in North America, the punk movement was spearheaded by a New York—based quartet called the Ramones. Onstage, the band resembled emaciated Muppets on speed, racing through such songs as "Blitzkrieg Bop" and "I Wanna Sniff Some Glue" without stopping for breath, as fans pogo-danced in frenzied unison. At one club, the entire audience started banging their heads against the floor in time to

the song "Suzy Is a Headbanger." Lead singer Joey Ramone commented that "It was like, really sick."

The punk movement paved the way for raw, gonad-driven acts of today like Guns N' Roses, Van Halen, and the Red Hot Chili Peppers. The Chilis are particularly creative in their stage assault, utilizing gimmicks such as fire-eaters, semi-nude dancers, and wire-suspended entrances. Another notable feature is lead singer Anthony Kiedis' ability to maintain headstands during bandmates' solos, should they prove tedious. There

Rock and Roll REVEALED

On the Road Again TOURING

*Below: Silent partners: Milli
Vanilli lip-sync to taped vocals
at a concert. Opposite: U2's
Bono as rhinestone cowboy.*

is also the infamous "sock stunt," in which band members appear for encores naked save for tube socks concealing their genitalia. At one Vancouver gig, police were mollified when assured that the Chilis were wearing G-strings with wires that kept the socks in place. But it ain't so; if the Chilis have any adhesive tricks, they're not saying.

In the eighties and nineties, R-rated theatrics have become part of the rock and roll mainstream. Madonna is the commercial queen of the genre; she has proved she can pace the nasty boys of rock shock for shock. Madonna pushes the envelope of good taste with her gender-bending costumes, simulated masturbation, and choreography that includes crotch grabbing and Nazi goose stepping. As early as her 1985 "Like a

Virgin" tour, Madonna titillated audiences by straddling a ghetto blaster and announcing, "Every lady has a box, but mine makes music." (Madonna's audacity was almost eclipsed on one tour, when opening act the Beastie Boys included a twenty-foot [6m] pink penis among their stage props.)

But one relatively tame Madonna move scored thirteen-year-old dancer Chris Finch major points in the eyes of his friends. Madonna had cast Finch as a sexually curious innocent in her "Open Your Heart" video, and hired him as a dancer for her "Who's That Girl?" tour. The choreography for the song "Like a Virgin" featured Madonna bestowing a brief kiss upon young Finch. When the show played Finch's hometown, Madonna surprised him with a

full-fledged smooch. Finch smiled as he recalled, "I lost my place and couldn't remember the steps in the number."

Protests against Madonna's show by Italian Catholics led to the cancellation of a Rome gig in 1990. Madonna responded to the censorship with a statement to the press: "If you are sure I'm a sinner, then let he who has not sinned cast the first stone."

Madonna and others have also been criticized for what they *don't* always do in show, that is, sing. A *Rolling Stone* exposé alleged that many top acts—including Madonna, Paula Abdul, Jody Watley, and George Michael, as well as Michael and Janet Jackson—often use prerecorded tracks.

George Varga of the *San Diego Union* renamed Madonna's "Like a Virgin" show "Like a Concert," noting: "For all intents and purposes, the concert *was* the record.... It's a fraud foisted on unsuspecting fans." Critic Jon Pareles of *The New York Times* posited that approximately half of the show's music was canned.

Milli Vanilli was said to lip-sync entire concerts. During one show, the computer malfunctioned, and the boys were caught gasping for song. They fled offstage just as the machine kicked on, blasting their vocals without them. But you can only get away with just so much. It was later discovered that Milli Vanilli didn't even sing on *Girl You Know It's True*, the album that won the group the Best New Artist Grammy in 1989. Milli Vanilli had to return the award, which evidently inspired them to prove that they are musical artists of some stripe. They released an album of their very own in 1993.

Similarly, New Kids on the Block met with reality while playing to a record executive convention in Florida. The Kids had forgotten to bring their "backing" vocal tape and had to depend on their own live pipes. "You could see the look of total panic on the guys' faces," recalls an attendee. "The lead singer actually ran offstage, he

Rock and Roll REVEALED

couldn't hit the notes. The Kids were trying to impress reps from worldwide labels, and clunking around and not being able to sing, they almost threw their career away."

In a bizarre reverse, original Pink Floyd singer Syd Barrett (who was later diagnosed as schizophrenic) refused to open his mouth at all while his pretaped voice sang "See Emily Play" during the band's 1967 appearance on *American Bandstand*.

Musician-producer Don Was cynically dismisses the problem of lip syncing: "People aren't going to shows to be absorbed in musical values, they're going to be in the presence of celebrity... the kinds of audiences the bands attract don't *care*—you just start the lights flashing, you don't even have to move your lips."

Indeed, even the top musical talents of rock—the ones who really do sing—are starting to get lost amid props, lasers, and video screens. At twenty dollars and up per ticket, the stadium performers feel compelled to cough up Broadwayesque extravaganzas. For the video generation, the music is no longer enough.

Now, performers such as the Rolling Stones, Prince, and Michael Jackson incorporate dancers and large horn sections to beef up their acts. Jackson's 1988 show even included entire miniballets, such as the gun-toting gangster scenario enacted to the song "Smooth Criminal." And Mick Jagger has outgrown the cherry picker he used to ride around in in days of yore—he must now have multilevel airport runways to strut on, to befit his supersonic stature. Even politically correct, band-of-the-people U2 have gotten glossy; their 1992 stages seemed engulfed by huge video screens, spitting out a barrage of video clips. Apparently the rock show slogan of the nineties is More Is More.

I WANT CANDY

Rock Star Perks and Quirks

Michael Jackson: Once fretted that something was wrong with the water at London's posh Claridge's Hotel and insisted that hundreds of bottles of Perrier be heated to fill his tub.

Elton John: Insists all plastic flowers be replaced with real ones.

Madonna: Must have a trunk full of penny candy—especially Hot Tamales—in her dressing room.

Stevie Nicks: Can't abide greens or oranges in her hotel room's decor.

Prince: His hotel suites must be draped in soft, flowing fabrics and smell of his favorite incense upon his arrival.

Ratt: Must have a hundred condoms supplied at each tour stop.

Rolling Stones: Once had the walls of a Madrid hotel torn down to make the band's suites larger (and heaven forbid Keith gets a larger suite than Mick, or vice versa).

Steven Tyler: In his wild-man days, Tyler insisted that backstage buffet tables never include turkey roll, only real turkey. Tyler was known to overturn entire tables full of food if he spotted the dreaded turkey roll.

Van Halen: Must have M&Ms in their dressing rooms, but all the brown ones must be removed.

ZZ Top: Must have an "Elvis shrine room with dimmer" backstage, where they can feel they are one with the King before they perform.

Tommy Can You Hear Me?

THE FANS

Teenyboppers they're not: Hell's Angels await a Stones show in London's Hyde Park.

Many fans are content just to be in the same room with their rock and roll idols. But others are not content until they obtain a personal audience.

Gavin DeBecker has made a career out of protecting stars from overzealous admirers. According to *Rolling Stone*, In fact, DeBecker has special classifications for mentally unbalanced fans. Categories include "'special powers' (the fan believes he's directed by God), 'religious obsession' (the fan believes he is God), 'science fiction' (the fan believes

aliens have landed), 'debt-owed' (the fan believes he wrote a hit song and deserves royalties) and 'out of control' (the fan believes his movements are directed by a radio transmitter implanted in his brain)."

DeBecker's most famous case involved a fan who was obsessed with Olivia Newton-John. The fan was thwarted in his attempts to reach Newton-John, but later succeeded in killing his own parents. A search of his personal effects indicated that he was planning to murder U.S. Supreme Court Justice Sandra Day O'Connor.

Mick Fleetwood remembers a rather strange, obsessive fan who once confronted him with one of Fleetwood Mac's album covers. "See that photo?" said the fan. "It might be your head, but it's my torso."

It's generally believed that the Rolling Stones made a big mistake when they hired the Hell's Angels to protect them from fans at the infamous Altamont concert. The film *Gimme Shelter* documents the tragic event that occurred there. The chorus of the song "Gimme Shelter," is "Rape! Murder! It's just a shot away!" On that day in 1969, murder was just a knife away.

The Angels had plunged into their work with savage glee, keeping the peace by beating audience members with clubs. Teeth were knocked out, jaws were broken; scores of Stones fans were bruised and bloody. Then, as the band launched into "Sympathy for the Devil," an eighteen-year-old African-American man named Meredith Hunter pulled out a pistol in an attempt to defend himself in some way against a

Rock and Roll REVEALED

biker who had slashed him in the back. (Meredith was at the concert with his white girlfriend; the biker apparently objected to interracial dating.) The Angels, however, knew an opportunity when they saw one, and chose to interpret Hunter's act of self-defense as a potential threat to Jagger.

They surrounded Hunter, took away his gun, and began stabbing him in the face and back. He fell to the ground. Angels began to kick him, crushing his nose and jaw. Finally, a steel bucket was twisted into his face until he took his last breath.

Keith Richards was asked later about the actual police's response to the murder. "The cops had disappeared; they didn't want to know s--t," claims Richards. "...As far as they were concerned, one kid got born there, one died there, so there was the same amount of people who came out as went in.... It was chaos."

Sometimes the violence rock music inspires in fans is of a more solitary, personal nature. In the early nineties, both Ozzy Osbourne and the band Judas Priest faced charges of subliminally inciting the suicides of two teen fans.

In 1990, two separate cases were filed against Osbourne and CBS records. Both cases involved boys who shot themselves in the head apparently soon after listening to Osbourne albums that included the song "Suicide Solution." Ben Mills, the attorney for both sets of parents, alleged that the recording contained the subliminal directive "Why

try, why try, get the gun and try it." Osbourne's side denied the existence of such a message, and pointed out that one of the boys had a history of drug and alcohol problems, and the other had been drinking at a party where he was spurned by a girlfriend. In May 1991, the suits were dismissed.

In the Judas Priest case, two teens shot themselves—in an apparent pact—after an afternoon of drinking beer, taking drugs, and listening to the album *Stained Class*. One boy died instantly, the other suffered extensive facial injuries. Three years later, in an alleged suicide, the second boy overdosed on prescription medicine.

The prosecution claimed that one song on the album, "Better by You, Better by Me," was embedded with the instruction "Do it." Judas Priest member K.K. Downing commented, "It will be another ten years before I can even spell 'subliminal.'"

One young friend of the deceased told a reporter that he had sold the teens drugs. "I sold them acid all the time," he said. "They were tripping for about a year before this happened. No way was it the music." The defense played on the drug-use evidence and also suggested that both boys had somewhat checkered family histories. The sister of the boy who died instantly admitted on the stand that, although she didn't listen to heavy metal music, she too had twice tried to commit suicide. The suit against Judas Priest was ultimately dismissed.

However, heavy metal songwriters now admit that they're starting to think twice about their influence on their audience. Guns N' Roses guitarist Slash says, "If some guy goes out and kills his girlfriend, that's gonna f--- my head up. I mean, this is serious. It's affecting the lives of people you don't even know, which is definitely a scary thing, to have that much power."

How ironic that songwriters who start out wanting to be taken seriously often end up wishing their fans would heed Mick Jagger's reminder: "It's only rock and roll."

Chapter Two

Honky Chateau

HOME LIFE

Prince's Paris pad is

located within this

modest dwelling on

Avenue Foch.

Just plain folks: Paul, Linda, and James McCartney grocery-shopping on Long Island during a 1981 vacation.

Imagine singing to fifty thousand screaming fans who know every word of your lyrics. Imagine the limos, the popping flashbulbs, the groupies who thrill to your very presence, the endless perks. Now imagine returning home from a tour to an empty house or a wife or husband who feels ignored, a baby that needs changing, bills that need paying—the dreaded stuff of real life. It's no wonder rock stars cram their home lives with toys, luxuries, and hobbies. What else can take the place of quasidivine adulation?

Even more so than actors, many rockers still live out the classic rags-to-riches fantasy. Hence, once they make it big, they can't get enough of the good life, glutting themselves with expensive cars, mansions, servants, pools, clothes, and lovers—a kid's-eye view of success. As decorator-to-the-stars Phyllis Morris comments, "Rock people are just like the movie stars of the forties. It's exciting to watch them spend money. They're looking for something that says they've just arrived. They're creative, emotional, uninhibited. And in

their homes you'll find an atmosphere of uncontrolled funk." Spell "funk" with an "O," as in ostentation. Many rock stars' tastes veer giddily back and forth between Sotheby's high style and Las Vegas bordello.

It's hard to believe (at least when compared to today's real estate prices) that Elvis Presley bought Graceland for $100,000 in the late fifties. From the outside, the place appears to be a stately southern mansion, with Georgian columns and graceful shade trees. The "Music Gate" at the front, a double gate adorned with guitars and musical notes, is a charming touch of whimsy. The decor inside, however, is not exactly subtle.

Elvis' decorating taste favored red, pink, purple, and gold; mirrors; shag carpets; and lots of velvet. The music room, where Elvis spent hours at his grand piano, was done entirely in red. "Natural" was not in the King's decorating vocabulary; the drawing room features fake gilded seventeenth-century furniture with red velvet upholstery, a large fake fireplace, and bookshelves filled with fake books. Elvis' bedroom was done in a red-and-black Spanish motif, with cerise drapes and a black padded door. In Elvis' day, the centerpiece of the master bedroom was a nine-by-nine-foot (2.7 × 2.7m) custom-made bed, which required custom-made sheets. Two television sets were embedded in the ceiling so the King could watch without sitting up. For when he deigned to sit, there were televisions stationed at the foot of the bed. A large refrigerator yielded cool treats such as Pepsi and ice cream.

Graceland has been open as a tourist attraction since shortly after Presley's death. Many of the rooms seem a museum preservation of a certain style of seventies decorating, of the chrome, vinyl, and Dacron variety.

The seventies were certainly a heyday for displays of opulence among the rock and roll set. Whereas the sixties had focused a bit more on the pop star as happy-go-lucky flower child, by the seventies rockers were becoming deal-wise, landowning adults. Rod Stewart and girlfriend Britt Ekland epitomized the glamorous rock couple of the period. They decorated their Los Angeles spread à la Art Nouveau, with paintings selected at Sotheby's, linens and kitchenware from London and Hong Kong, and extravagant lamps and candelabra flown in from Paris. Even when dining alone at home, the flaxen-haired duo would dress in full evening attire.

Many rock stars hung their hats in Los Angeles homesteads in the seven-ties. Linda Ronstadt, Robbie Robertson, Mick Jagger, and Ron Wood all had Malibu mansions during this time, and many more greeted the new day from perches high in the Hollywood Hills. Eagles Don Henley and Glenn Frey shared a swinging bachelor pad in the Hollywood Hills in the mid-seventies. In Joe Smith's book, *Off the Record*, Henley looks back on the pair's Odd Couple life-style, recalling, "I was sort of the housekeeper, the tidy one. He was the lovable slob. All around the house he'd leave these little cigarette butts standing on end. They looked like miniature cities. Burns all over the furniture and carpet, coffee cups all over the place. We would get up every Sunday, watch football together, scream and yell, and spill things."

While the home of the Eagles sounds like a prime-time sitcom, the seventies domain of bluesman John Mayall was strictly X-rated. Mayall prided himself on his extensive pornography collection, which included a huge erotic painting on the bottom of his swimming pool and an alphabetized pornography library. The collection, inherited from Mayall's father, featured

When Elvis was in residence, a constant coterie of fans waited at Graceland's "Music Gate" for a glimpse of the King.

Mick Jagger's cozy French hideaway.

photographs, postcards, and literature dating back as far as the Victorian era. The material was lost in a fire in 1979.

Another Los Angeles resident, Keith Moon, kept up his hellion image at home. On a lark, Moon once destroyed neighbor Steve McQueen's carefully tended sapling copse with his motorcycle. Record producer David Geffen summed up the rock-star life-style at the time in *Time* magazine: "Rock performers don't talk to artists or economists. As a group,

they are a collection of narcissists in desperate need of a catalyst. A rock performer goes to a friend's house to smoke dope. They listen to each other's music and feel special. The guy goes home telling himself he's had a night on the town."

In the eighties and nineties, both road and home life appear to have calmed considerably for pop musicians. Particularly in England, many rock and roll animals are now indistinguishable

from old money country gents. Roger Daltrey tends the trout fishery on his estate in Burwash, England. Eric Clapton is captain of the local cricket team in Cranleigh. Steve Winwood enjoys the occasional pheasant hunt. George Harrison is an avid gardener, and has designed his grounds in a classic seventeenth-century style. Ever-genteel crooner Bryan Ferry sips tea daily with his wife, Lucy, and their four young sons in their antique-laden home.

Rock and Roll REVEALED

Over in London, Elton John's mansion shows few traces of the glittery excess that made the singer famous. Like any good English aristocrat, John reveres his dogs, and indeed has a cemetery for departed pooches—with little headstones that read Bruce, Brian, etc.—on his grounds.

Many of the top wage earners of the music industry can, of course, afford several homes. If Mick Jagger and Jerry Hall had put as much work into their

WORKING IN A COAL MINE

Former Jobs

Pat Benatar: Bank teller
Jon Bon Jovi: Burger King employee
David Bowie: Model, art teacher
Belinda Carlisle: Gas station attendant
Elvis Costello: Computer programmer
Roger Daltrey: Sheet-metal worker
Terence Trent D'Arby: Army corporal
Jon Elliot: Van driver
Peter Gabriel: Travel-agency assistant
Bob Geldof: Pea sheller in a factory
David Gilmour: Model
Darryl Hall: Apple picker
Hammer: Oakland A's bat boy
Debbie Harry: Playboy Bunny
Chris Isaak: Tour guide in Japan
Mick Jagger: Ice cream vendor
Dr. John: Ivory Soap baby
Jon Knight (New Kid): Burger King employee
Cyndi Lauper: Racehorse walker
Simon LeBon: Lumberjack
Annie Lennox: Fish filleter in a factory
Madonna: Artist's model
George Michael: Movie usher
Bette Midler: Go-go dancer
Keith Moon: Plaster salesman
Vince Neil (Mötley Crüe): Electrician
Stevie Nicks: Hostess at Bob's Big Boy restaurant
Elvis Presley: Usher, truck driver
Lou Reed: Assistant in an accounting firm
Keith Richards: Ball boy at a tennis court
Nikki Sixx (Mötley Crüe): Worked at Music Plus in Glendale, California
Rod Stewart: Gravedigger
Sting: Schoolteacher
Donnie Wahlberg (New Kid): Shoe salesman
Tom Waits: Vacuum-cleaner salesman
Peter Wolf: Radio DJ

relationship as they have into buying and remodeling houses, they might not have suffered such tribulations. At last count, the on-again, off-again pair claimed four major residences: in London, New York, France, and the Caribbean island of Mustique.

The London and New York places reveal Hall's knack for shrewd antique shopping. As Hall explained in a 1988 spread in *Architectural Digest*, "I don't really like modern things. I wanted the [New York townhouse] to be cozy and luxurious, and I don't find modern interiors either cozy or comfortable." Hence, Hall haunts European house sales, picking up a William VI sideboard here, a Louis XV sofa there, eighteenth-century fashion prints, ottomans, tapestries, paintings—all adding up to what a *House and Garden* reporter referred to as a look of "stylish clutter."

Clutter was what Jagger and Hall wanted to avoid in the design of their

island getaway. When they seek serenity and simplicity, the couple can truly seclude themselves on the three-mile (4.8km)-long Grenadine island, whose only access is a charter flight from Barbados. It took five years to complete the compound, called Stargroves. Several Japanese pavilions adjoin the original cottage. Walkways lead to guest rooms, the bath house (with hot tub), a game room, and the children's cottage, where progeny Elizabeth, James, and Georgia sleep. The objets in the main house have been chosen with care, and include personal items such as family pictures and exotic knickknacks from Far East vacations.

Both Jagger and Hall seem to revel in their luxury homes. Both came from moderately humble beginnings: Jagger from middle-class London and Hall from suburban Mesquite, Texas. Now a top-tier gentlewoman, Hall has truly come a long way from Mesquite to Mustique.

Above: Gloria Estefan's sunshine estate in Miami. Right: Ozzy Osbourne relaxes at his house in Los Angeles.

Rock and Roll REVEALED

Another star with a penchant for interior design is the ever-profligate Cher. The restless pop diva—actress recently gave up her Egyptian-style compound in Beverly Hills because "I was too content there." Her early nineties decorating project is a Malibu house, complete with pool, jacuzzi, and tennis court. The beach house has a comfortable, cushiony feel—lots of leopard-skin print garnished by the star's collections of crucifixes and snake effigies. Cher notes, "I would have loved being a decorator. I love looking at fabrics and colors, the way objects take up space."

Indeed, Cher's designer pal Ron Wilson believes the star keeps moving simply because she enjoys decorating.

Not every rock star takes such joy in ascending to the coveted house on the hill. In 1990, Guns N' Roses front man Axl Rose had a two-bedroom house built for himself and then-wife, Erin Everly (daughter of Don Everly, of the famous Everly Brothers). Rose visited his home-to-be one night when the decorating was nearly finished and experienced a crisis of alienation. Says Rose, "I'm standing in this house going, 'This house doesn't mean anything to me.

This is not what I wanted. I didn't work forever to have this lonely house on the hill that I live in because I'm a rich rock star.' So I shoved the [$38,000] piano right through the side of the house." Rose then proceeded to trash the fireplace and a statue, and break all the windows. The ultimate tab in damage: $100,000. Poor little rich boy.

Axl Rose settles in for a quiet night at home.

MY MASERATI DOES 185

Cars

Paula Abdul: Jaguar
Bono: Mercedes
David Bowie: Volvo
Roland Gift: Saab
Darryl Hall: Jeep
Hammer: Porsche
Mick Fleetwood: Jeep
Janet Jackson: Mercedes
Mick Jagger: Ferrari
Elton John: Bentley
Madonna: Mercedes, Thunderbird
Paul McCartney: Mercedes
Michael McDonald: Chevy truck
George Michael: Mercedes
Mike Mills (R.E.M.): Thunderbird
Elvis Presley: Cadillac, Mercedes

fans and acting for a movie camera. Sting, Roland Gift, Art Garfunkel, Roger Daltrey, and, most notably, Cher and David Bowie, have all received positive reviews for their screen work. Others, like Madonna and Mick Jagger, are still struggling to hit it as big on celluloid as they have on acetate.

One of the top-grossing actor-rockers of his time was Elvis Presley. Although Presley received praise for his natural acting ability, he was extremely embarrassed by his on-screen image. According to biographer Red West, the King would bristle: "Who is that fast-talking hillbilly sonofabitch that nobody can understand? One day he is singing to a

Fifty-seven Channels (and Nothing On)
PASTIMES AND PURSUITS

Above: *Spandau Ballet's Gary and Martin Kemp impressed critics with their film turn as murderous brothers in* The Krays.

Right: *Sting appeared as the sinister Feyd-Rautha of House Harkonnen in David Lynch's 1984 film epic,* Dune.

After the decorating's done, there are non-musical hours in the day to fill up. Rock star pursuits range from leisurely—gardening for Belinda Carlisle, painting for Paul McCartney and Ron Wood—to serious moonlighting. For several years now, Jethro Tull leader Ian Anderson has led a double life as a musician—salmon farmer. Anderson admits that it took awhile for him to gain the respect of his angling colleagues, but he is now taken seriously in the fishery industry. Observes Anderson, "I don't find the idea of being a musician getting in the way, except when I have to say, 'OK', to the people who work for me, 'you're on your own for a few months. I'm off to make another record.'"

Similarly, many musicians split their professional lives between singing for dog, then to a car, then to a cow. They are all the same damned movies with that southerner just singin' to something different." Certainly films like *Kissin' Cousins, Fun in Acapulco,* and *Viva Las Vegas* were little more than formulaic star vehicles. Elvis' manager, Colonel Tom Parker, wasn't kidding when he told a Twentieth Century-Fox executive, "Just send me a million dollars, never mind the script, and Elvis will do the picture." But once in a while, in films like *Kid Creole* and *Wild in the Country,* Elvis got to do some real acting; the critics responded favorably, and the King was quite proud.

Like Elvis, David Bowie has often been cast in roles similar to his stage persona. But unlike Elvis, that persona has often been far from the rock and roll mainstream, and an oeuvre of diverse and often bizarre characters has resulted. The former Ziggy Stardust has proved a chameleonlike actor, portraying an alien (*The Man Who Fell to Earth*), a vampire (*The Hunger*), and

a warlock (*Labyrinth*), as well as the occasional human being, with a flair. For his Broadway turn in *The Elephant Man,* Bowie received critical raves, and a crossover star was born.

Another star who has made the transition from music to film is Cher. Unlike Madonna, Cher has rarely taken a false cinematic step, appearing in a string of critical hits such as *Silkwood, Mask,* and *Moonstruck.* Cher admits that she has occasionally had trouble giving up the rock star trappings and inhabiting less luminous characters. When she was called upon to portray a drab-dressing lesbian in *Silkwood,* she burst into tears at the sight of her wardrobe. "You have to understand," she told director Mike Nichols, "it's going to be very hard for me not to look good."

Cher was looking good when the critics praised her work in 1985's *Mask.* But when she was passed over for an Academy Award nomination, Cher protested by arriving at the Oscar ceremony dressed in a very revealing—

Biblical Bowie: *The former Thin White Duke dons Roman robes for his role as Pontius Pilate in Martin Scorsese's* **The Last Temptation of Christ** *(1988).*

CELLULOID HEROES

Match the Movie With the Star

A. Bowie	1. *Catch-22*
B. Cher	2. *The Wall*
C. Phil Collins	3. *McVicar*
D. Roger Daltrey	4. *Freejack*
E. Art Garfunkel	5. *Dogs in Space*
F. Bob Geldof	6. *Mermaids*
G. Debbie Harry	7. *Runaway*
H. Michael Hutchence	8. *The Man Who Fell to Earth*
I. Mick Jagger	9. *Buster*
J. John Lennon	10. *Hairspray*
K. Madonna	11. *Dracula*
L. Prince	12. *Mad Max 3: Beyond Thunderdome*
M. Gene Simmons	13. *How I Won the War*
N. Sting	14. *A League of Their Own*
O. Tina Turner	15. *Under the Cherry Moon*
P. Tom Waits	16. *Dune*

A8; B6; C9; D3; E1; F2; G10; H5; I4; J13; K14; L15; M7; N16; O12; P11

Answers

Cher garnered an Academy Award nomination for her portrayal of an Oklahoma nuclear factory worker in 1983's Silkwood.

and costly—spider woman from Mars outfit. But Cher hung in there, and the hard work paid off when she won an Oscar for *Moonstruck* in 1987.

Another of Cher's media roles is that of fitness diva, joining stars like Jane Fonda in the quest for the perfect bod. In the eighties, many rockers traded in nightclubs and whiskey for gyms and Perrier. As Sting puts it, "You have to have a certain amount of vanity to get onstage. If I don't think I look good, I don't perform very well. If I'm fit, toned up, don't look tired, and I've done some preparation, I perform better. People pay money to see you, so if I had to perform tonight, I'd be going through a certain regime—work out, take a bath, don't eat any rubbish, get a good night's sleep."

That's certainly a change from survival-of-the-fittest partying days of the seventies. Most rockers have daily exercise regimens, and many tour kitchens are strictly sprouts and veggies. Gone are the days of Elvis' cheeseburger binges; Madonna, Chrissie Hynde, Paul McCartney, and Michael Jackson all insist on vegetarian catering for their tours. Hynde is a particularly vocal anti-meat activist who once refused to go onstage until an ad for a burger chain was covered up. Fumes Hynde, "I think killing an animal and eating it is like eating your own child."

Some rockers' newfound dietary evangelism stems from past eating disorders. Elton John now admits to having been bulimic, a condition he believes he suffered largely due to concern over getting fat. Recounts John, "For breakfast I'd have an enormous fry-up...then a tub of Häagen Dazs vanilla...[then throw up]...if I was eating a curry, I couldn't wait to throw it up so that I could have the next one."

John now strictly adheres to three meals a day, does not snack, and eats no sugar or white flour. But some old-timers still keep the torch of dietary indulgence burning: Jerry Lee Lewis attributes his continuing vitality to a diet

I WANT TO GET PHYSICAL

Workouts

Paula Abdul: Bike riding
Belinda Carlisle: Jogging, tennis, mountain biking
Stewart Copeland: Horseback riding, polo
Bruce Dickinson (Iron Maiden): Fencing
Sammy Hagar: Boxing
Chris Isaak: Surfing
Mick Jagger: Jogging
Gary Kemp (Spandau Ballet): Mountain climbing
Madonna: Jogging, swimming, dancing, weight training
Aimee Mann: Softball
Ted Nugent: Hunting, chopping wood
Elvis Presley: Karate
David Lee Roth: Rock climbing, martial arts
Mike Rutherford (Genesis, Mike and the Mechanics): Horseback riding, polo
Sting: Jogging
Suzanne Vega: Dancing

Rock and Roll REVEALED

BLACK COFFEE IN BED

Favorite Food and/or Drink

Jon Bon Jovi: McMuffins; Tequila Slammers
Bobby Brown: Seafood
Cher: Chocolate
Phil Collins: Sashimi
Terence Trent D'Arby: Brown rice
Mick Jagger: Apple pie
Elton John: Indian food
Simon LeBon: Angel hair pasta with porcini sauce
Madonna: Chocolate sundaes
Paul McCartney: Linda's vegetarian quiche
Michael McDonald: Mexican food
Joey McIntyre (New Kid): Mexican food
George Michael: Sweet-and-sour pork balls
Jim Morrison: Jack Daniel's
Elvis Presley: Cheeseburgers
Keith Richards: Rebel Yell and Jack Daniel's

Rocker fuel: Jerry Lee Lewis toasts a successful gig at New York's Lone Star Cafe in 1987.

of malted milk, shrimp, scotch, and "almighty rock and roll." Jimmy Cliff has a much simpler health philosophy: "Keep a cool head, eat well, and have free bowels—then you'll live as long as you want."

Speaking of longevity, Michael Jackson's reported doings, habits, and interests have provided fodder for the gossip-hungry and kept the tabloids buzzing for over a decade now. Did Michael really propose to Elizabeth Taylor? Did he try to chemically bleach his skin? Did he really try to buy the remains of the Elephant Man? Does he take hormones to maintain his soprano vocal range? Does he sleep in a hyper-

baric oxygen chamber that he believes will extend his life? Is he gay? How many of his facial features have been surgically altered?

Manager Frank DiLeo will confirm only a friendship with Taylor, the bid for the Elephant Man's bones, and Michael's nose and chin jobs (he denies rumors that Michael had his eyes and cheekbones done.) Michael's mother insists that the vocal register is a family trait. Brother Marlon asserts that, in the Jackson 5's touring days, Michael's (hetero)sexual prowess was "something to keep up with." As for the bleached skin rumor, there's no actual evidence, although a quick look at old

album covers such as *Off the Wall* and recent releases, such as *Dangerous*, is enough to raise eyebrows.

In a recent interview with Oprah Winfrey, however, Michael attempted to set the record straight. He said he didn't own any of the Elephant Man's bones, didn't sleep in an oxygen chamber, and didn't bleach his skin but suffered from a genetic disease that caused his skin pigment to deteriorate. He declined to discuss his plastic surgery and his sex life (although he did say he had been dating Brooke Shields).

But Michael's childlike and semi-paranoiac shyness are more than just rumors. Now in his early thirties, he

Does he or doesn't he? Michael Jackson's extreme physical transformation over the years has given rise to rumors of extensive cosmetic surgery and skin bleaching.

leads a reclusive life at his northern California ranch, "Neverland." He is devoted to his many pets, which include a llama, a giraffe, an Arabian stallion, a lion, various snakes, and lots of exotic birds. Jackson's favorite pet is Bubbles, a chimpanzee who can ride a horse, roller-skate, and moon-walk. Michael's pastimes have been perfect to share with pals like Emmanuel Lewis and Sean Lennon—when they were children. But Quincy Jones defends Jackson's innocence: "He's just got a very pure enthusiasm for simple things."

In his interview with Oprah, Michael admitted his behavior was a result of having missed his actual childhood, as he fronted the family act from age five. And if sister LaToya is to be believed, all the Jackson children suffered both physical and psychological abuse from their ruthlessly ambitious parents, particularly their father. (Michael confirmed his father's abuse in the Oprah interview, but described his mother as "perfection.") It is the combination of such emotional scarring and the lifelong place in the center spotlight that has caused Michael to withdraw into his own private world. Of all of the major stars who participa-

ted in the "We Are The World" video, Michael Jackson was the only one who insisted on taping his segment alone in another studio.

Despite his eccentricities, the King of Pop has found a way to make his life and music work. He is a truly charitable man, frequently inviting groups of underprivileged and ill children to his home for barbecues, and donating sizable sums to orphanages, hospitals, and the United Negro College Fund. In a business that is rife with drug casualties, promiscuity, and general lunacy, Jackson's singular image is almost refreshing. According to Quincy Jones, "Michael Jackson is grounded and centered and focused and connected to his creative soul. And he's one of the most normal people I've ever met." In the world of rock and roll, normal is truly a relative term.

Rock and Roll REVEALED

The former Cat Stevens now sings only songs of Islamic worship.

Till I Reach the Higher Ground

SPIRITUAL INTERESTS

Contrary to popular belief, not all rock musicians are beer-guzzling heathens. Many have found strength in faiths as disparate as the many styles of popular music. Elvis, the Beatles, and Pete Townshend all followed Indian gurus at one time. Bob Dylan has tried on several different religions. Prince's entire career is a wild Ping-Pong between sex and religion.

Jerry Lee Lewis, cousin of preacher Jimmy Swaggart, adheres to the Church of God Pentecostal faith. Ex-wife Myra took the brunt of Lewis' fundamentalist frenzy: "It was, 'Don't go to the movies because if you do, you go to hell'; 'Don't wear diamonds 'cause it's a sin'; 'Jezebel painted her face, so don't put makeup on.' It's a shame. The man is tortured. Jerry thinks that Jerry is too wicked to be saved."

Eric Clapton, on the other hand, did find salvation in Christianity. As the story goes, two Christians came backstage after a 1969 Blind Faith concert and asked Clapton if he'd like to pray with them. Always open-minded, Clapton acquiesced and got down on his knees. It felt good. After the prayer, he got to talking with his new friends. Somehow, the conversation got onto Jimi Hendrix, and Clapton offered to show them his favorite poster of Hendrix. Clapton unrolled the poster; inside was a poster of Christ that he'd never seen before. He converted to Christianity on the spot. Clapton's faith has certainly been tested over the years, beleaguered as he has been by tragedy. (See pages 55 and 84.)

The classic tale of rock and roll conversion involves the former Cat Stevens, now Yosef Islam. His epiphany occurred during a near-drowning accident on a California beach in the mid-seventies. Stevens promised God that if he was spared, he would devote himself to spreading the Word. Suddenly, a strong wave arose and pushed him back to shore. "God never forgets," says Stevens. "If somebody makes a promise, that promise, in God's sight, has to be fulfilled." When Stevens became a Muslim in 1979, he gave away everything he owned: his guitars, gold records, and the like. He's now married and the father of five children, and spends his days running a Muslim school near London.

Michael Jackson is another of the faithful. The Gloved One actually used to go door to door—in disguises like austere suits, hats, and false mustaches—spreading the word of the Jehovah's Witnesses. Jackson's star status stirred up the faith so much that one faction began to believe Michael was a kind of Messiah, and referred to him as the "archangel Michael." (Leaders of the faith frowned on this development.)

At the other end of the religious spectrum is Irish singer–media event Sinéad O'Connor. In October 1992, O'Connor capped a career rife with political petulance by ripping up a picture of Pope John Paul II on a live television broadcast of *Saturday Night Live*. Pronounced O'Connor, "Fight the real enemy." O'Connor later explained that she felt Roman Catholicism was at the

Rock and Roll REVEALED

root of the child abuse she had suffered. Regardless, many found her expression of protest inappropriate: she was booed off the stage at a concert tribute to Bob Dylan two weeks later, and even the ever-inflammatory Madonna denounced O'Connor's action.

Not all rock stars' spiritual beliefs involve organized religion; several prominent stars are rumored to dabble in the black arts. The most notorious of these is Led Zeppelin's Jimmy Page. In the Zeppelin biography *Hammer of the Gods,* former Page girlfriend Pamela Des Barres submits, "I believe Jimmy was very into black magic and probably did a lot of rituals, candles, bat's blood, the whole thing. And of course, the rumor that I've heard forever is that they all made this pact with the Devil, Satan, the Black Powers, whatever, so that Zeppelin would be such a huge success. And the only one who didn't do it was John Paul Jones. He wouldn't do it. Who knows where the rumor came from? But that was the rumor." The rumor went on to suggest that the band's string of bad luck—Robert Plant's auto accident, the death of Plant's young son, the death of drummer John Bonham—

were part of the payment for the band's superstardom. Page will only allow, "I'm attracted to the unknown."

Other bands, such as Black Sabbath, have used Satanic images as attention-getting gimmicks. Sabbath's original lead singer, Ozzy Osbourne, claims that the band was never actually into black magic, and that the demonic mystique was just another well-calculated rock and roll package. Archbishop John Cardinal O'Connor did not take the stratagem so lightly, and in 1990 accused Osbourne and other rockers of creating music that "is a help to the Devil." Osbourne defended his lyrics, denying charges of Satanic exhortation and attributing his dark outlook instead to his bleak upbringing in industrial Birmingham, England.

The Rolling Stones have also incorporated an element of Mephistophelian mystery into their image. The album title *Their Satanic Majesties Request* set the ball rolling in 1967, and Mick Jagger's eerie rendering of the song "Sympathy for the Devil" the following year, compounded the demonic mystique. Writer, filmmaker, and Stones friend Kenneth Anger reveals that

Jagger eventually became very uncomfortable about the Stones' Satanic connection: "He thought that it was too heavy. When he married Bianca, he was wearing a rather prominent gold cross around his neck." However, Anger firmly believes that Stone Brian Jones was a witch. Anger claims Jones revealed an extra nipple, on his inner thigh, as evidence of his otherworldliness. "In another time, they would have burned me," said Jones proudly.

Another pop musician with an attachment to the netherworld is Stevie Nicks. Nicks wrote one of her biggest hits, "Rhiannon," about a witch, and subsequently called her publishing company Welsh Witch Music. Nicks believes in magic, reincarnation, and ghosts. And she also claims that Halloween is her favorite night of the year. Says Nicks, "If ghosts are friendly and willing to talk, I am ready to sit down at any time. I would love to."

Stranger things have happened in the world of rock and roll.

Left: Stairway to Hell? Rumors of demonic dabbling surround former Led Zeppelin guitarist Jimmy Page. Below: Paint it black magic: Rolling Stone Brian Jones believed he was a witch. Opposite: Irish singer-songwriter Sinéad O'Connor has a bone to pick with the Catholic Church.

Chapter Three

Hope I Die Before I Get Old
DRUGS

Draw a picture of the stereotypical rock star, and what do you include? Skintight pants, at least one tattoo, a lightning bolt—shaped guitar, wild, teased hair, snakeskin boots, a bottle of booze, and of course, the requisite cargo of pharmacological goodies. Oral histories of popular music suggest that the majority of rock and roll performances—live and recorded—were rendered under the influence of intoxicants.

Are drugs and rock and roll perpetually yoked? And which begat the other? Did rock music lead innocent youth toward stupefied decadence, as the Elvis-hating Holy Rollers of the fifties warned, or was rock music born of some roots bluesman's narcotic reverie?

In his book on the Rolling Stones, *Symphony for the Devil*, Philip Norman reminds us that drugs did not spontaneously appear when Bill Haley first sang his hit, "Rock Around the Clock."

In the Victorian era, Norman notes, London was "the drug capital of the Western world." Opium lozenges were a very popular cough remedy, and even by the mid-twentieth century, heroin and cocaine could be obtained by prescription. As Norman asserts, "Hard drugs…had been an upper-class pursuit long before pop musicians started giggling over marijuana."

Of course, not every rocker was handed his or her first illegal substance

Rock and Roll REVEALED

by another musician. While in the army, Elvis Presley was introduced to Dexedrine, a stimulant that became one of his favorite drugs. (A sergeant used to give Elvis' unit the drug to help the soldiers stay awake for extended maneuvers.) After his return to civilian life, Elvis continued to take the pills regularly. Problems arose when, after indulging his new fondness for uppers, the King needed something to help him relax, whereupon he began experimenting with barbiturates and tranquilizers (his favorites included Quaaludes, Tuinal, Placidyl, and Seconal). As the years went by and Elvis developed various health problems—including digestive disorders and hypertension—his medicine cabinet filled up with drugs of all sorts. An ironic footnote of Elvis' last decade was his appointment by Richard Nixon as an honorary narcotics agent for a federal antidrug campaign in the United States.

It is common knowledge that drug abuse fueled the King's final decline. Friends say Elvis seemed relatively happy during the last week of his life. He swam and played racquetball daily; he seemed enthusiastic about an upcoming tour; and he was enjoying a visit from his daughter, Lisa Marie. However, insiders believe that Elvis was depressed due to the recent publication of a tell-all book written by his former bodyguards that detailed his drug problems and fits of temper. The King felt betrayed by the members of his inner circle, and turned to—what else?—more drugs.

At 2:30 P.M. on August 16, 1977, Elvis keeled over in his bathroom at Graceland. Apparently he had been sitting on the toilet reading a book entitled *The Scientific Search for the Face of Jesus*. He was rushed to Baptist Memorial Hospital in Memphis, but he died an hour later. A hospital employee reported, "Elvis had the arteries of an eighty-year-old man [Elvis was forty-two at the time of his death]. His body was just worn out." The coroner ruled death by

natural causes, but some time later, a hospital spokesperson commented that the actual cause of death was "polypharmacy," that is, chemical damage caused by combining too many types of pills for too long.

The King may be dead, but his memory lives on. Every year on the anniversary of his death, Graceland is inundated with floral remembrances from around the world. As night falls, dedicated fans conduct a somber candlelight procession.

Elvis once said that the secret to happiness is having "Something to do, something to look forward to, and someone to love." Elvis had lost the love of his life, Priscilla—she left him for his karate instructor (see page 79)—and perhaps, somewhere in a mountain of prescription vials, his sense of purpose.

Another drug "casualty" of the early years of rock and roll is James Brown. Although Brown is alive and continues to record and perform, a multidecade drug habit has taken its toll on him. One particularly lurid episode occurred in 1988, when Brown, high on PCP and wielding a shotgun, burst into an insurance seminar that was taking place in a building that was adjacent to his Augusta, Georgia, office. Brown wanted to know who had been using his private toilet and began firing questions at seminar leader Geraldine Phillips. "I thought if I answered one of those questions wrong, he was going to kill me and everybody else," said Phillips. It was later discovered that the shotgun didn't even work.

Finally, someone managed to slip out of the room and call the police. When the patrol cars arrived, Brown hopped into his car, and the chase was on. Brown led the law across state lines to South Carolina, where he allegedly tried to run over two policemen as they were setting up a roadblock. Officers shot out Brown's front tires, but he was able to drive another six miles (9.6km) before his truck hobbled into a ditch. As

police tried to administer a sobriety test, Brown broke into his stage routine, singing "Georgia" and doing his "Good Foot Dance." He was booked, then released on bail; within twenty-four hours he was arrested again for driving under the influence of PCP. In 1988, the Godfather of Soul was sentenced to six years in a South Carolina prison, although he was recently paroled under a work-release program.

In the early sixties, parents who clucked their tongues over the likes of leering, sneering, gyrating Elvis welcomed the new arrivals from Britain, those innocent boys next door, the Beatles. But John Lennon once claimed that there wasn't a single phase of Beatledom that didn't feature one drug or another. He said, "... *A Hard Day's Night* I was on pills. I started on [them]... when I was seventeen, since I became a musician. The only way to survive in

James Brown once told an employee, "I got the Lord in one hand and the Devil in the other."

Hamburg, to play eight hours a night, was to take pills. The waiters gave you them—the pills and drink.... *Help!* was where we turned on to pot, and we dropped drink, simple as that. I've always needed a drug to survive. The others, too, but I always had more, more pills, more of everything because I'm more crazy probably."

The Beatles' *Sergeant Pepper*/LSD period began when a dentist friend slipped the hallucinogen into John's and George's coffee at a dinner party. The two guitarists began to take acid regularly, and psychedelic images began to emerge in Beatle lyrics. Lennon noted that Paul and Ringo tried the drug but didn't like it as much. (However, Paul has been arrested for marijuana possession many times since then, and Ringo is now a recovering alcoholic.)

About 1966–1967, John began to have more and more "bad trips," and completely lost his sense of self: "I didn't think I could do anything. I was s--t. Then Derek [Derek Taylor, the Beatles' public relations man]...said, 'You're all right,' and pointed out which songs I had written: 'You wrote this,' and 'You said this,' and 'You are intelligent, don't be frightened.'"

Looking back on that period in a 1971 interview, Lennon submitted his view of the correlation between drugs and rock music, "It was only another mirror. It wasn't a miracle. It was more of a visual thing and a therapy, looking at yourself a bit.... But it didn't write the music. I write the music in the circumstances in which I'm in, whether it's on acid or in the water."

In the mid- to late sixties, acid was an integral part of the Great (social) Revolution. Timothy Leary urged the youth of America to "Turn on, tune in, and drop out," and Ken Kesey spiked the Kool-Aid at his notorious San Francisco Bay Area "acid test" parties.

Peter Albin of Janis Joplin's band Big Brother and the Holding Company remembered a typical San Francisco music festival scene: "I remember after playing a disjointed set, we got off, and some girl started taking off her clothes and some guy started passing around a bucket of ice cream laced with acid, and the place just started vibrating." Similarly, Jefferson Airplane/Starship's Grace Slick recalled an acid test held at a ranch in Marin County: "Neil Cassidy [writer Jack Kerouac's sidekick] was high on acid and holding forth. Twelve or so people were sitting in a circle listening to Neil's acid rap. Someone was painting the side of a bus. Another person was reading somebody's aura. Other people were upstairs making

love. I'm sure there are parties that go on now that are similar to that—the outfits are different."

Slick's song "White Rabbit" was believed by some to be a drug anthem and was banned by some stores and radio stations. But Slick commented: "'White Rabbit' was directed not to the kids but to the parents. People think I was exhorting all young people to take drugs. We already were taking drugs. I didn't have to exhort the young people. I was telling the older people, 'This is what we're doing and why we're doing it.' You tell us not to take drugs, and

yet you read us books—when we're very young—like *Peter Pan*, which says sprinkle something on your head and you can fly, books like *Alice in Wonderland*, where she takes at least five different drugs and has a wonderful time. What do you think you told us? That a chemical is going to get you where you want to go.'"

The house band at Kesey's party was usually the everlasting Grateful Dead. For close to thirty years now, the Dead have been seen as the vanguards of psychedelic rock. It seems appropriate that Jerry Garcia took the band's

name from an Egyptian prayer, as the band has flowered into something of a religion. Legions of devoted fans, called Deadheads, plan their lives around the Dead's touring schedule, dropping out of school, quitting jobs—whatever it takes to sustain their obsession. And although most Dead lyrics don't specifically condone drug use, most of the fans' eyes at Dead shows tend to look a little glassy. But do the band members themselves practice what their music seems to preach? In a 1980 *Rolling Stone* magazine interview, Jerry "Captain Trips" Garcia observed, "It's

The Jefferson Airplane epitomized the psychedelic San Francisco music scene in 1968.

always been part true and part false. It's never been anything but something you do in addition to playing music. The fundamental thing we're doing is being a band, not selling or promoting drugs...none of us takes drugs regularly. I think drugs are just a reality of American life in one form or another, I mean, hell, they're there."

They were definitely there when the band was arrested on drug charges in New Orleans while rehearsing songs for their album *Workingman's Dead*. The Bourbon Street bust was later immortalized in the Dead song "Truckin'."

One of the highlights of the acid rock era was the Monterey Pop festival in 1967. That concert introduced the world to two exciting new performers,

Jimi Hendrix and Janis Joplin. Both were talented, exciting blues rock interpreters; both were bright, vulnerable drug abusers; and both died in the autumn of 1970.

Jimi Hendrix grew up in Seattle, learning his chops in the local blues joints, buoyed by liberal quantities of Benzedrine and codeine-based cough syrup. As Hendrix's star rose in the basement cafes of New York, his constant companion was a baby bottle filled with methedrine-spiked water. Marijuana, LSD, and cocaine use followed, and as the sixties drew to a close, Hendrix was flying high. In Victoria Balfour's book *Rock Wives*, Leslie Meatloaf (yes, Meatloaf's wife) remembers her three-day "date" with Hendrix during 1969's Woodstock festival, "Just being around him, you could get high by osmosis. He was like an acid trip—he just took everything. At that time, people used to throw pills onstage, and little bags of marijuana, and you wouldn't know what was in these pills. He used to have a roadie gather it all up and bring it to his room, and he'd sort through it and take whatever. Another thing that he enjoyed doing would be to take a can of Hawaiian Punch and throw a lot of acid in it and leave it in the refrigerator."

Hendrix's signature song, "Purple Haze," was inspired by a little purple pill that he popped one night at a club gig. After his set, he floated offstage and penned the lines that include "'Scuse me while I kiss the sky." Hendrix once tried to explain his state of mind: "Craziness is like heaven. Once you reach that point where you don't give a damn about what everyone else is sayin', you're going toward heaven. The more you get into it, they're going to say, 'Damn, that cat's really flipped out. Oh, he's gone now.' But if you're producing and creating, you know, you're getting closer to your own heaven. That's what man's trying to get to, anyway."

As 1969 drew to a close, Hendrix was quite far from heaven. He had

been charged with drug smuggling by Canadian border officials and feared a seven-year jail sentence (he was later acquitted), a former colleague had sued him for breach of contract, his record royalties were in escrow, a large portion of his earnings could not be accounted for by his management, the building of his dream recording studio—Electric Ladyland—was running over budget and behind schedule, and one of his girlfriends, Devon Wilson, was getting more and more into heroin. Jimi felt he had been betrayed by those he trusted, and his mood was sour.

On September 2, 1970, Hendrix gave a concert in Denmark. His strange behavior there revealed how depressed he was. Just after playing a wailing version of "In From the Storm," he said to the audience, "I've been dead a long time," and immediately walked offstage. End of show.

On the night of September 17, 1970, Hendrix went to a dinner party with some friends. The group indulged in Chinese food, various pills, and powdered "Owsley Sunshine" LSD. Hendrix's friend Monika Dannemann came to pick him up, and the two returned to her apartment. The details of what followed are hazy, but it is generally believed that Hendrix ingested up to nine sleeping pills with red wine. The barbiturates paralyzed Hendrix's cough reflexes, and early on the morning of September 18, he was asphyxiated by his own vomit. Biographer David Henderson hastens to point out that Hendrix never abused heroin, but regardless, the guitar picneer clearly succumbed to the excesses of his generation.

Hendrix will forever be linked with his spiritual sister Janis Joplin, who gave in to her demons two and a half weeks after he did. Janis Joplin was an anomaly in her time: a young white woman who sang the blues. But both her full-tilt, intemperate, emotionally tortured life and her shabby, untimely demise were well in keeping with the melancholy music she adopted. Janis told a

Hope I Die Before I Get Old  51

and driving dry-cleaning trucks while I'm making $50,000 a night." But there was cold comfort in revenge; she had always felt like an outsider and could never find the acceptance she craved.

Janis played the wild mama role with a flair—getting arrested for using obscene language onstage, bellying up to bar after bar, helping herself to male groupies—but inside she was deeply insecure, particularly about her looks. She usually hated the way she looked in photographs.

In March 1969, Janis' picture was supposed to have appeared on the cover of *Newsweek*. However, former U.S. president Dwight D. Eisenhower died that week, and he appeared on the cover instead. When Janis was shown the flattering picture of herself that was to have hit newsstands across the United States, she was incensed: "Goddamnit, you motherf---er! Fourteen heart attacks and he had to die in MY week!"

The most enduring image of Janis Joplin is of a smiling, befeathered, thrift-store waif clutching her ever-present bottle of Southern Comfort. John Phillips said that Janis once confided in him that her bottle often contained not liquor but—echoing Hendrix's teen predilection—codeine cough syrup. But it was harder stuff than either of these that silenced Janis' voice once and for all. In October 1970 Janis' inert body was discovered in a room at the Landmark Hotel in Hollywood. Friends said that Janis had seemed happy; the singer was at work on a new album and engaged to be married. But on October 4, she injected a lethal dose of heroin into her veins and became another rock and roll statistic.

Ironically, shortly after her death, "Me and Bobby McGee," a track from the new album, became Joplin's first number one hit. Janis' voice sang out from radios around the world, "Freedom's just another word for nothing left to lose." Dead at twenty-seven, she was finally free.

reporter sometime in 1968, "I never seem to be able to control my feelings, to keep them down...my mother would try to get me to be like everyone else...And I never would....It tore my life apart. When you feel that much, you have super-horrible downs.... Now, though [in the band], I've made that feeling work for me....Maybe I won't last as long as other singers, but I think you can destroy your now by worrying about tomorrow."

Janis Joplin was a prodigal daughter of Port Arthur, Texas. She never felt like she fit into the Texas high school football/cheerleader hierarchy; her classmates whispered about her oddball clothes and promiscuity, and she threw it back in their faces with wild behavior and profanity. Shortly before her death in 1970, she attended her high school reunion, as she said, "just to jam it up their a--es, [just to] see all those kids who are still working in gas stations

They say bad luck comes in threes. Indeed, out on the town with friends in late 1970, Jim Morrison liked to say "You're drinking with Number Three." He was right.

Morrison grew up in a military family in California and Alexandria, Virginia. Young Jim was an avid reader who noted the substance abuse of favorite writers such as Brendan Behan, Dylan Thomas, and Baudelaire. When it came time to name his rock band, Morrison looked to a psychedelic literary granddaddy, Aldous Huxley. Morrison paraphrased Huxley's book *The Doors of Perception* when he explained his band's name: "There's the known. And there's the unknown. And what separates these two is the door, and that's what I want to be."

According to biographers Jerry Hopkins and Danny Sugerman, Morrison was already "gobbling acid tabs like beer nuts," and plowing through mountains of Mexican marijuana at the band's genesis. Doors drummer John Densmore said about Morrison, "He really wanted to get out of himself, totally go to the ends, as far as you can go, every time."

By 1967, Morrison had settled on alcohol as his intoxicant of choice. He commented to a friend, "I'm getting good at it. . .every sip is another chance. Another flashing chance at bliss." Two years later he amended his initial view: "You're in complete control. . .up to a point. It's your choice, every time you take a sip. You have a lot of small choices."

Morrison may have been the sex symbol of his generation, but his drunken antics were usually not cute. On one occasion, he shared a bottle with Janis Joplin at a Hollywood party. Suddenly he turned mean. He grabbed Joplin's head, forced it into his crotch, and held it there. The vulnerable Joplin finally broke away and ran into the bathroom crying.

At another party, Jim passed out drunk in a chair and urinated on the rug. Toward the end of his life Jim confessed that he drank to cope with the pressure he felt, and added: "I think drinking is a way to cope with living in a crowded environment and also a product of boredom...I hate the kind of sleazy, sexual connotations of scoring [drugs] from people, so I never do that. That's why I like alcohol. You can go down to any corner store and it's right across the table."

Jim continued his legendary binges when he moved to Paris in the spring of 1971, just a few short months before his death. On one occasion, he allegedly fell out a hotel window, landed on top of a car, bounced off, got up, dusted off his clothes, and strolled away to get a drink.

On July 3, 1971, Morrison's girlfriend Pamela Courson found him dead in the bathtub of their Paris apartment. A rescue team could not revive

"I think the highest and the lowest points are the important ones. All the points in between are, well, in between. I want freedom to try everything—I guess to experience everything at least once."

—Jim Morrison

SHE DON'T LIE

O.D. Heaven

John Bonham: September 25, 1980

Paul Butterfield: May 4, 1987

Brian Cole (The Association): August 2, 1972

Pete Farndon (The Pretenders): April 14, 1983

Jimi Hendrix: September 18, 1970

James Honeyman-Scott (The Pretenders): June 16, 1982

Janis Joplin: October 4, 1970

Frankie Lymon (Frankie Lymon and the Teenagers): February 27, 1968

Phil Lynott (Thin Lizzy): January 4, 1986

Robbie McIntosh (Average White Band): September 23, 1974

Keith Moon (pictured): September 7, 1978

Brent Mydland (Grateful Dead): July 26, 1990

Jon Jon Paulus (The Buckinghams): March 26, 1980

Bon Scott: February 19, 1980

Sid Vicious: February 2, 1979

Alan Wilson (Canned Heat): September 3, 1970

him; the Lizard King was gone at the age of twenty-seven. A quick autopsy and burial spurred suspicions (par for the course with rock stars) that Morrison was not really dead, but had faked his death to escape the pressures of pop fame. The official statement by Doors manager Bill Siddons claimed that Jim "died peacefully of natural causes." Opposing factions favor heroin and cocaine respectively (combined with alcohol) as the true cause. In Joe Smith's book *Off The Record*, Doors guitarist Robby Krieger offered his opinion: "The last time I saw Jim Morrison was right before he left for Paris…. He was coughing up blood. This is my own theory of how he died, but I think it would have been very easy for him, after a night of drinking, to take a couple of snorts of something and not know what it was.

Jim could do that, take a big snort. And then maybe just go into the bathtub, fall asleep, and drown."

Morrison was buried in the Père Lachaise Cemetery in Paris, among other notables such as Marcel Proust, Honoré de Balzac, Oscar Wilde, Sarah Bernhardt, and Jean-Baptiste Molière. A plethora of spray-painted messages, most of which are accompanied by an arrow that point the way to "Jim" or the "Lizard King," adorn the cemetery walls and other people's tombstones. The marker on Morrison's grave is a statue of the singer's head; the statue sits on the ground, and is surrounded by bottles of Jack Daniel's and beer, syringes, and bongs—all of which have been wedged into the dirt.

The triple loss of Jimi, Janis, and Jim provided a dark transition from the

Rock and Roll REVEALED

*L*eft: Clapton slipped into abusing drugs thinking they might enhance his guitar playing. But usually when he played back tapes made during his stoner years, they sounded lousy. The only exception was "Layla," recorded while the entire band was high. Opposite: Jim Morrison's grave, Père Lachaise Cemetery, Paris.

idyllic Summer of Love era to the war-torn, hard-rocking early seventies. Joplin's good friend Nick Gravenites shed light on the scene at the time: "This whole rock scene…it's like a prison, really…there's a lot of people using junk in the rock scene, and they're on death row, the rest of them are on Tier C. The ones that abuse themselves the most in terms of hard drugs, or really excessive anything, drinking or whatever, they're automatically put on death row. It's just a way of enduring because you know they're going to die, you know it. So [their friends] are just figuring out ways to cushion the blow when it happens."

Gravenites' prison metaphor was particularly apt for guitar great Eric Clapton, who went into self-imposed seclusion from December 1970 to the beginning of 1973. In interviews with biographer Ray Coleman, Clapton refers to the combination of the pressures of fame, his unrequited love for Pattie Boyd Harrison (Beatle George Harrison's wife), the recent deaths of Hendrix and his own grandfather, and an impulse to explore the depths of heroin as the reason for his retreat. Clapton offered this analysis of this troubled period in his life: "There was definitely a heroic aspect to it. I was trying to prove I could do it and come out alive. At no time did

I consider it suicidal or shutting down on life. The rejected love affair, the apparent non-availability of Pattie, was a factor. I had to prove to myself that I could do this thing on my own—that I could forget Pattie, survive, and come back from the dead."

Just before he closed the doors, Clapton had had his entire band, Derek and the Dominoes, living with him. The band rehearsed twenty-four hours a day while doing acid, pills, cocaine, and marijuana, then crashed and started all over again. Clapton claims that the group's cocaine dealer insisted they buy heroin along with the cocaine, as he needed to get rid of it. The heroin piled

Hope I Die Before I Get Old

up in one of Clapton's drawers for a while, but finally Clapton became curious. "I liked it...when it wore off, I didn't feel too bad either, and so I did it for maybe a year, very infrequently, also doing lots of coke and other drugs and drinking as well."

Clapton credits his emergence from heroin purgatory to Pete Townshend. The two guitarists had not been particularly close friends, but as Clapton said of Townshend, "...he's a great humanitarian and cannot stand to see people throw their lives away."

Townshend spent long hours talking to Clapton, soothing his middle-of-the-night panics, and trying to reach him and convince him to get clean. Thinking a return to work would be the best medicine, Townshend planned a charity concert that would feature Clapton. The show was scheduled for January 13, 1973, and included Townshend, Steve Winwood, and Ron Wood. Five minutes before the show was to start, Clapton still had not arrived. Townshend said he went out onto the back stairs of the concert hall and prayed, "Please God,

make Eric come before the show...." Clapton arrived one minute before the performance was to begin. He said he was late because his white suit had needed letting out (due to two years of binge eating). He went onstage, and, fortunately, the comeback was a stunning success.

Of course, one concert didn't make for a miracle cure. Clapton went to live at the home of Dr. Meg Patterson for twenty-four-hour recovery supervision. Patterson practiced neuroelectric therapy that involved Chinese principles of acupuncture. A special device attached to an electric stimulator was clipped onto Clapton's ear for daily treatments. He kept busy during the day by playing his guitar and making car and airplane models. Clapton was able to withdraw from heroin under Patterson's care; when he left, he gave her a gold spoon for sniffing heroin that he had worn on a necklace for the previous three years. His note read, "Thanks, Meg. I won't be needing this."

Unfortunately, the road after heroin addiction did not lead straight to sobri-

ety: Clapton began to drink to fill the void heroin had left him with, and like "everything else," Clapton said, he "did it one thousand percent." Ironically, Pete Townshend became his hard-drinking buddy; in the early seventies, Townshend's alcohol intake had gone up to two bottles of brandy a day, and Clapton edged ever closer to his friend's prodigious consumption. In fact, on his first big tour after kicking heroin, Clapton remembers being "so drunk on some stages that I was lying...flat on my back or staggering around wearing the weirdest combination of clothes because I couldn't get it together to dress properly." And his life continued on in this extremely debaucherous manner throughout the seventies.

But by 1980, Clapton's body was starting to show signs of the abuse. He had developed a nagging back pain that year. In keeping with his self-destructive bent, he went on tour and, to keep going, simply took forty to fifty painkillers a day—in addition to his daily bottle of brandy. He played a Wisconsin concert doubled over in pain; he was clearly in serious trouble. As he and his band flew to their next tour date in Minneapolis, Clapton's manager, Roger Forrester, saw that the musician was just slumped over in his seat and, most eerily of all, not drinking. When the plane landed, Forrester rushed Clapton to a nearby hospital. X rays revealed that Clapton had a huge ulcer that was just about to explode into his pancreas. Forrester wanted to fly Clapton home to England for treatment, but the doctor stopped him because he believed that Clapton's condition was life-threatening. Later, after treatment, doctors admitted to Clapton that he'd probably had about forty-five minutes to live when he was first hospitalized.

In January 1982, Clapton checked into a clinic to dry out. He said he remembered the bizarre feeling of watching television with his fellow alcoholics and seeing his Michelob beer commercial. It was a revelation to him to live in

barracks-type accommodations, to make his own bed, and to do community chores all day.

Yet, for the first part of his stay, Clapton secretly felt he was just playing for time, doing what was expected of him to get through the ordeal. But his breakdown and subsequent break-through came when Clapton was given a detailed questionnaire that had been filled out by his wife, Pattie (who had by then divorced Harrison and married Clapton—see page 84). Pattie had responded to questions like, "Did your husband ever rape you? What was he like when he was drunk?" Clapton admitted that Pattie had responded to the questions in ways that made him finally realize that he'd "behaved like an animal." He said, "...that's when I cracked.... Once I'd broken down I felt a lot better, although it did hurt me very deeply.... What was left was a very insecure human being, a little bit frightened of the outside world."

Since that time, Clapton has maintained sobriety with help from support groups, his religious faith (see page 41), and his music. His newfound strength has certainly been tested, plagued as he has been with recent tragedies such as his young son's fatal fall from a Manhattan high-rise and the helicopter crash that took the lives of his personal bodyguard, assistant tour manager, and booking agent, as well as guitarist Stevie Ray Vaughan (see page 64). Clapton may well be rock and roll's most remarkable survivor.

Another rocker in that league is Papa John Phillips of the Mamas and the Papas. Phillips' autobiography, *Papa John*, is a roller-coaster ride from the dizzying heights of pop-idol status to semihuman junkie catatonia.

With the success of songs like "California Dreamin'" and "Monday Monday," the Mamas and the Papas skyrocketed to stardom in the mid-sixties. Parties at the Phillipses' Bel Air mansion featured a pool table evenly covered with a rainbow assortment of

pills. Guests could simply take whatever they wanted; experimentation was encouraged. Phillips wrote of the period: "I volunteered my body as a human test tube for anything I could get my hands on—mescaline, Black Beauties to keep going, Reds to come down, hash and grass for any occasion. A friend of ours once brought over a box of free drug samples he had taken from a doctor's office. I went through everything in there, including the female hormone, estrogen.... [His former wife, Mama Michelle] asked me if I was preparing to go through menopause. 'No, but there's probably a little downer buzz in there....'"

John's children from his first marriage, Jeff and Laura (known to television viewers as MacKenzie Phillips of the hit series *One Day at a Time*), came to live with him in 1972, at the apex of the druggie era. Papa John laid down the law to his then-thirteen-year-old

daughter regarding her curfew: she could stay out until 1 A.M. on school nights, 5 A.M. on weekends, and could stay out all night only once a week. Jeff and Laura stole marijuana and then cocaine from their father's stashes. Jeff got so he needed a "wake-up toot" of cocaine just to get him going in the morning. When Jeff spent a successful summer at music camp, John "rewarded" him with a stash of cocaine and a few joints.

Eventually, Michelle left Phillips. He subsequently married Genevieve Waite, a woman whose drug tolerance easily matched his own. Phillips also found another partner in crime in Keith Richards; the two became cadaverous soul brothers. At their junkie worst, Keith and then common-law wife Anita Pallenberg moved in with the Phillipses. Keith and John would record music, but Anita rarely left her room. According to Phillips, Anita "lit candles, sobbed,

A family affair: John Phillips shared his love of recreational drugs with wives Genevieve Waite and Michelle Phillips, and daughter MacKenzie. Phillips remembers celebrating one "white Christmas" by snorting cocaine with his family.

snorted coke, cooked shots of heroin, and was in agony." Apparently, the Richardses' young son, Marlon, was afraid to leave his parents alone for fear of what might become of them. Eventually, the music suffered, too. John wrote that a typical Richards-Phillips night in the recording studio in the midseventies consisted of getting "loaded," and then spending the "entire night either in the bathroom or tuning our guitars and trying to remember what song we were working on."

By Christmas 1977, John Phillips had become a full-fledged heroin addict. In *Papa John*, he writes of sitting by his swimming pool in Los Angeles, watching his youngest children, Tam and Chynna (now a member of the band Wilson Phillips), and Marlon Richards run around the yard shooting each other with "water pistols" that were actually Phillips' syringes.

In addition to heroin, Phillips was also injecting cocaine, which was making him hallucinate. He believed that

tiny white bugs were crawling around under and on his skin. He was so certain they were real that he had friends and family look for them. He treated himself with ointments and flea powder, but the bugs wouldn't go away. A friend tried to trick him psychologically, suggesting he wrap himself in a suit made of something akin to plastic wrap; when the bugs appeared, the friend suggested, Phillips could quickly peel off the suit—wiping the bugs off—and throw it into the furnace. Phillips tried it, but the bugs were too clever for him. A psychiatrist friend tried to tell Phillips that there were no bugs crawling on him, but that he was "stark raving crazy" and needed help. Ultimately, though, Phillips' remarkable physical tolerance and determination to keep the "human test tube" going won out: the bugs went on their merry way, allowing him to keep his internal laboratory running as smoothly as ever.

At one point, Phillips did commend himself and his wife into the hands of a

doctor for detoxification. This extremely expensive program took place in an isolated, rural area in the southern United States. Several bodyguards were hired to keep the couple from sneaking drugs into the complex. As soon as the doctor left the complex on other business, one of the guards asked Phillips if he could get him some Quaaludes. Phillips said he could, and the guard promptly put him on a plane for New York City. Phillips soon returned to the hospital with both the Quaaludes and a fresh supply of his own drug of choice, Dilaudid, picked up his wife, and terminated the "cure."

Phillips' spree finally ended with a jail sentence for narcotics. In his autobiography Phillips claims that he then cleaned up, got therapy for himself and his family, and returned to the original high—his music. However, in July 1992, Phillips underwent a life-saving operation. On the brink of death, suffering from advanced cirrhosis and chronic hepatitis, Phillips had a liver transplant, as his liver had been destroyed by years of drug and alcohol abuse. Photographs of the singer revealed that Papa John looked old enough to be someone's great-great-grandpapa.

Phillips' pal Keith Richards has been a little luckier. When Richards says, "I come from very tough stock and things that would kill other people don't kill me," it's not a boast but a simple statement of fact.

The Rolling Stones were encouraged by manager Andrew Loog Oldham to embody rock and roll darkness in all its various avenues of excess. Over the Stones' thirty-odd years, Richards evolved from the geeky, jug-eared second guitarist (behind the flashier Brian Jones) to a reptilian rock pirate, earring and skull ring flashing as his searing riffs propelled the band to superstardom. And his cadaverous look in the seventies was not just an act: by the beginning of the decade, Richards had graduated from pill-popping neophyte to bona fide junkie.

Rock and Roll REVEALED

Like their friends the Phillipses, Richards and Anita Pallenberg were a couple who brought out the addictive worst in each other. Both their son, Marlon, and daughter, Dandelion, were born while Anita was addicted to heroin. In 1970, Richards evaded British tax collectors by moving his family to the French Riviera. In a case of creative smuggling, he had his heroin shipped to him on a regular basis inside toys for his children. Richards refers to the mid-seventies as "that period of moral ambivalence," and admits that "it got to a point where the music became secondary. I was devoting most of my time to scoring and taking dope." In an attempt to clean up for a 1973 tour, Richards went to Switzerland and underwent a forty-eight-hour blood transfusion—

supposedly a cure for heroin addiction. The cure seemed to work, but Richards couldn't stay away from narcotics, and the drug haze continued.

The party came to an end in 1977, when Toronto police found twenty-two grams of heroin in Richards' hotel room. Keith and Anita finally submitted to drug rehabilitation, and the guitarist was let off with probation and a charity performance for the Canadian National Institute for the Blind.

By the eighties, Richards was a new man (although he still chain-smokes Marlboro reds and claims to favor champagne), taking more control in the Rolling Stones and branching out into solo projects. On his birthday in 1983, he married actress-supermodel Patti Hansen in Cabo San Lucas, Mexico,

with Mick Jagger on hand as best man. Richards and Hansen subsequently settled in Manhattan (they now own residences in Paris, Connecticut, England, and Jamaica as well) and started a family, which so far includes daughters Theodora and Alexandra. "Believe it or not," says Richards, "this is the way I always dreamed married life should be. I never have the chance to get bored with it, because I never really get enough of it. I'm away a lot. And, because of that, I never mind coming back to an active nest." A cozy finale for one of the darkest narratives in the world of popular music.

Keith Richards may have been a rock prototype of decadence, but many others have tried to claim his throne. The seventies punk movement begat

Below, left: Junkie parents Keith Richards and Anita Pallenberg with eighteen-month-old Marlon at their French villa. Below, right: New life-style, new family: Richards with wife Patti Hansen, mother of the couple's young daughters.

movie, *Sid and Nancy*. The pair were a kind of obnoxious, drug-addled Romeo and Juliet, hopelessly self-destructive but deeply in love. Nancy, originally from Pennsylvania, had dropped out of the University of Colorado and become a go-go dancer in New York. She was already using heroin when she hooked up with Vicious on a trip to London. The two became inseparable, and Nancy turned Sid on to the hard stuff. When the Sex Pistols broke up in 1978, Sid and Nancy moved to New York City and began their final decline.

The gory details of the night of October 11, 1978, in the couple's room at the Chelsea Hotel are unclear. But the next day, police found Vicious sitting dazed in the blood-splattered room. Nancy lay in the bathroom, murdered via stab wounds to the stomach. The rumor quickly spread that Nancy had wanted to end her miserable life and

Tainted love: Sid and Nancy, (above, in early 1978) loved each other, but they loved drugs more. When Nancy was found dead in room 115 at New York City's Chelsea Hotel later that year, she was naked save for a black brassiere.

many faux Richardses, boozing, swaggering, and veering between fame and tragedy. Punk laureates the Sex Pistols became acquainted with both.

In 1977, the Sex Pistols were the lewdest, crudest act in rock and roll. The brainchild of master media manipulator Malcolm MacLaren, the Sex Pistols were styled to exemplify every middle-class parent's nightmare. Johnny Rotten, Sid Vicious, Steve Jones, and Paul Cook brawled onstage, spat at their audiences, used the "F" word on television, and generally thumbed their noses at the British Establishment. They also abused every intoxicant they could get their hands on. It was the combina-

tion of addiction, encouragement to personify excess, and true love that spelled the end for bassist Sid Vicious.

The jury's out on how Sid—born John Simon Ritchie—got his menacing moniker. Some say it evolved from the time Vicious chain-whipped a journalist during his first gig with the band (although by that time he had already played drums with Siouxsie and the Banshees). Others say it was meant to be ironic—Sid was the sweetest punk bassist in the biz. But whether or not he was a fighter, he was certainly a lover.

Sid's relationship with his American girlfriend, Nancy Spungen, is compellingly chronicled in Alex Cox's 1986

60   Rock and Roll REVEALED

had begged Sid to kill her. Regardless, Vicious was booked for the murder. The *New York Post* offered an opinion with their headline: "Vicious: He Finally Lived Up to His Name."

But Sid's case never went to trial. Four months later, alone in his New York City apartment, Sid joined Nancy by way of a heroin overdose. This sordid finale was a fitting end for the ultimate punk.

After the degenerate seventies, it seemed like everyone in rock was just saying no; the eighties arrived with totems like squeaky-clean MTV vee-jays and bubble-gum bands like the Go-Gos and Wham! So it came as a great surprise that one of the most playful of the rock-lite acts, sweet transvestite Boy George, was a heroin addict. Like many rockers before him, the star attributes his habit to the strain of sudden fame. Also like others before him, George

started with marijuana, pills, and cocaine. "Whenever I had a moment of doubt, I would swallow a load of pills," he recalled. But George tried to maintain his impish MTV image. Even after police raided his house, George insisted, "I'm a drag addict, not a drug addict."

The breakup with his longtime lover, Culture Club's drummer Jon Moss, steered George toward harder stuff. By 1984, George was spending $750 a day on drugs for himself and hangers-on. The overdose deaths of two close friends finally woke him from his smack stupor. One, American musician Michael Rudetsky, had flown to London to play on George's solo album. One night after a rehearsal, Rudetsky stayed alone at George's Hampstead home while the singer went out to a nightclub. When George returned at 5 A.M., he found the keyboardist's lifeless body on the floor. Rudetsky had overdosed on heroin.

After that trauma, George sought the help of Dr. Meg Patterson—the aforementioned doctor who helped Eric Clapton—and cleaned up his act. By the late eighties, George claimed to be off of everything but the occasional tranquilizer. But it hasn't been easy; as he said, "When I'm on my own I cry. I cry all the time. But if I'm really unhappy I go and see my psychiatrist."

Boy George wasn't the only cuddly eighties pop star to belie his image. The ultimate girls-next-door, the Go-Gos, led a life-style in the early eighties that could give the early Stones a run for their money. In hindsight, Go-Go songwriter Charlotte Caffey reveals that she was either drunk or on drugs while writing almost every song and playing almost every gig of the Go-Gos' career. On one occasion, she was actually thrown out of Ozzy Osbourne's dressing room for being too rowdy. By the time the band broke up in 1985, she knew she needed help. "My life was at a very scary point," says Caffey. "I was very out of control as far as drinking and drugs, and I knew I had to do something, because I was going to die." She checked herself into a rehabilitation center and regained control of her life.

Singer Belinda Carlisle was also quite the party girl. Belinda feels she succumbed to the romantic stereotype of the screwed-up rock musician, justifying her life-style with her occupation. By 1985, Carlisle dried out, lost a lot of weight, found her Romeo (husband Morgan Mason, son of actor James Mason), and now has a flourishing solo career. Now, she says, old acquaintances whisper that she must have gotten cosmetic surgery, because she looks so much better. "But no," she laughs. "It's just living right."

Not everyone in rock and roll is in step with the current health craze. Since 1987, Red Hot Chili Pepper guitarist Hillel Slovak, Grateful Dead keyboardist Brent Mydland, former New York Dolls guitarist Johnny Thunders, and Will Shatter of Flipper have all overdosed.

Below, left: Boy George on stage in 1986, in one of many comeback attempts. It wasn't until 1992 that George's star rose high again with his rendition of the theme from the movie The Crying Game.

In particular, Seattle seems to be an opiate lovers' hub. Seattle denizens Andrew Wood of Mother Love Bone and Stefanie Sargent of Seven Year Bitch recently overdosed, and there have also been rumors of heroin abuse by the city's most famous nineties success story, Nirvana. Allegedly, lead singer Kurt Cobain and his wife, Courtney Love, lead singer of the all-woman band Hole, were both jacked up on heroin when Nirvana played a *Saturday Night Live* gig in January 1992. Unbelievably, Love supposedly (and unabashedly) continued her heroin abuse through the first few months of her pregnancy; miraculously, the child was born healthy.

Dave Mustaine of Megadeth has one explanation for the retro trend in drug use: "I was told I had to do heroin if I wanted to be great. I spent $500 a day for five years on freebasing heroin. If I hadn't screwed up like that, I'd be on easy street now." Mustaine got clean in 1990, and is thankful for his new lease on life: "The party's not over. The party's just starting."

After this litany of excess, it's refreshing to note that a few top stars—Tina Turner, Madonna, and Prince, to name a few—actually manage to fly high without the benefit of intoxicants. Bruce Springsteen accounts for his abstinence in this way: "I never did any drugs. When I was at that age when it was popular, I wasn't really in a social scene a whole lot. I was practicing in my room with my guitar. So I didn't have the type of pressure that kids might have today. Plus, I was very concerned with being in control at the time. I drink a little bit now. There's nights when I'll go out and do it up. But not too much when we're touring, because the show is so physically demanding, and you gotta be so prepared."

Ultimately, though, it's impossible to draw firm conclusions about the magnetic relationship between rock stars and drugs. Put simply, some stars use drugs and some don't. And some regret their stoner years and some don't. Jerry Garcia is one who doesn't regret his drug use: "It's one of those things where once in a while you want to blow out the pipes." But even the King of the Deadheads adds, "If drugs are making your decisions for you, they're no f---ing good. I can say that unequivocally. If you're far enough into whatever your drug of choice is, then you are a slave to the drug and the drug isn't doing you any good. That's not a good space to be in."

Garcia should know. In 1986 the guitarist collapsed and remained comatose, near death, for five days. The coma was attributed to a diabetic condition but was seriously aggravated by Garcia's past use of drugs. Only in the past year has Garcia become more careful with his health. But he's been successful—he shed fifty pounds (22.5kg) in 1992.

Ultimately, Garcia would probably agree with fellow drug veteran Keith Richards' take on tempting fate: "I've been closer to death a few more times than a lot of people. And what I've found out is that whatever it is, it's worth waiting for, you know?"

Pride of Seattle Kurt Cobain poses with progeny.

Rock and Roll REVEALED

Accidents Will Happen

FATAL MISHAPS

Not all rock and roll tragedies have resulted from overdoses. Although the rock and roll lifestyle may somehow have impaired the operation of planes, trains, and automobiles, sometimes rockers have just been at the wrong place at the wrong time.

Accidental deaths of beloved rockers are the most heartbreaking of all: a hardworking musician, often on his or her way to play for fans, suddenly plucked from the mortal world. Performers like Gloria Estefan and Billy Idol have cheated death in serious accidents; others have not been so lucky.

In his song "American Pie" songwriter Don McLean referred to February 3, 1959, as "the day the music died." That winter, a tour that included Ritchie Valens, J.P. Richardson (the Big Bopper), and Buddy Holly and his band, the Crickets, was basically a miserable bus ride through the northern Midwest. The buses were so drafty that one band member had to be hospitalized for frostbite. Every day, everyone layered on all the same clothes for warmth, and in close quarters, it was starting to stink. Holly felt responsible for his band's low morale. He promised that he would charter a plane to get them from Clear Lake, Iowa, to a warm, comfortable hotel in Moorhead, Minnesota.

When Richardson and Valens heard about the planned escape from the miserable bus, they bargained with Waylon Jennings (not a Cricket, but acompanying Buddy Holly on this tour) and Tommy Allsup for their seats on the plane. Allsup and Jennings grumpily deferred to the stars and the gang went on for the Clear Lake show. By all accounts, it was a rave-up: Holly, Valens, and Richardson sang together for fun, Buddy played drums for Dion and the Belmonts— everyone was in very high spirits.

At 12:40 A.M., the three stars arrived at the airport and boarded their plane. The little Beechcraft Bonanza took off, but the air-traffic controllers had made a tragic error: they had forgotten to notify pilot Roger Peterson of a special advisory that would entail flying strictly by instruments (not visually). The previous year, Peterson had failed his instrument certification test.

The plane disappeared into the night, pummeled by wind and snow. When the ground crew realized the Beechcraft had gone off course, they dispatched a search plane. Eight miles (13km) northwest of the airfield, the

pilot spotted the wreckage. The plane had hit a fence, sending Richardson forty feet (12m) in one direction and Valens and Holly twenty feet (6m) in the other. All were killed instantly.

Through the years, plane crashes have robbed the world of other great performers. In 1967, three days after Otis Redding had recorded the classic "(Sitting on) the Dock of the Bay," the singer's twin-engine Beechcraft went down in a Wisconsin lake. Jim Croce's plane crashed at the end of a Louisiana runway. Lynyrd Skynyrd's jet spiraled into a Mississippi swamp, killing Ronnie Van Zant, and Steve and Cassie Gaines. And former teen idol Ricky Nelson, on his way to a New Year's Eve gig, was killed when his DC-3 caught on fire and crashed in a Texas cow pasture. The night before, Nelson had performed at a club in Guntersville, Alabama. Ironically, the last song he had played was Buddy Holly's "Rave On."

One of the saddest reports in recent years was the August 1990 helicopter crash that took the life of Stevie Ray Vaughan. The brilliant guitarist had finally won his battle against alcohol and drug abuse, and had just won a Grammy for his album *In Step*.

On August 27, Vaughan and Eric Clapton played an outdoor arena gig in East Troy, Wisconsin. Eerily echoing the last-minute switches on Holly's plane, Vaughan had initially planned to drive back to Chicago with his brother and sister-in-law. At the last minute, Vaughan took the last remaining seat on the second helicopter of the Clapton entourage. The Bell Jet Ranger took off in a dense fog and, five minutes later, smashed into a man-made ski slope. The slope had no warning lights for aircraft; Vaughan, the pilot, and three of Clapton's employees were killed instantly. Clapton's own helicopter reached its destination safely. Federal

Aviation Administration records discovered after the crash revealed that the pilot had been involved in two previous aircraft accidents.

Many fatal accidents of rock and roll have occurred on the ground, too; automobile crashes have taken the lives of several rock greats.

Eddie Cochran was off to a terrific career start with hits like "Summertime Blues" and "Somethin' Else" when his vehicle crashed en route to a London airport in 1960; he was only twenty-one. Marc Bolan was killed in a car crash in the middle of a 1977 T. Rex comeback tour. And Harry Chapin, as famous for his humanistic political activities as for hits like "Taxi" and "Cat's in the Cradle," lost his life on the Long Island Expressway in 1981 on the way to a benefit performance.

In the Grateful Dead, the seat behind the keyboards seems jinxed. Original keyboardist Ron "Pigpen"

Rock and Roll REVEALED

McKernan expired of a liver ailment in 1973. He was replaced by Keith Godchaux, who died in a car crash in Marin County in 1980. Next came Brent Mydland, who overdosed in an apparent suicide in 1990. A truly spooky pattern for the ominously named group.

It was motorcycles, not cars, that proved to be the bane of the Allman Brothers. Early in 1971, Duane Allman said to Allman Brothers drummer Butch Trucks, "If anything ever happens to me, you guys better keep it going. Put me in a pine box, throw me in the river, and jam for two or three days." Did Allman have a premonition?

On October 29, 1971, Allman had visited band member Berry Oakley's house to wish a happy birthday to Oakley's wife. Allman got on his motorcycle to return home, and, riding as night fell, swerved to avoid a truck. But his motorcycle skidded, dragging him

fifty feet (15m). Allman's girlfriend and Oakley's sister had been following him in a car and cared for him while awaiting the ambulance. After three hours of surgery at Macon Georgia Medical Center, Allman died, at age twenty-four.

But the story gets even stranger: almost exactly a year after Allman's death, Oakley was riding his motorcycle through Macon when he slammed into a bus just three blocks from the site of Allman's accident. Oakley was also twenty-four. He was buried in the same cemetery as Duane.

Of course, some rock and roll accidents haven't required the operation of heavy machinery. Actually, it's hard to know whether to classify the death of Rolling Stone Brian Jones as accidental, for it seems as if Jones spent most of his life rehearsing for the end.

Brian Jones put the Rolling Stones together in 1962, and was originally the most popular member among female fans. He was the most distinctive-looking of the group, with his blond hair and flair for fashion. Onstage, he was the coolest of the early Stones, blasting great blues licks on his guitar while maintaining an icy demeanor. But

those close to the band knew the aloof air was a mask for a struggle for self-control. Jones was asthmatic and terribly allergic, and throughout every stage performance, terrified of the onset of an asthma attack. The myriad pills he took to maintain his health set a pattern of drug dependence that plagued him throughout his life.

His relationships with the other Stones were also a source of difficulty for the sensitive Jones. Although he had started the group, the focus quickly shifted to charismatic Mick Jagger. By the time Jagger and Keith Richards had been established as the band's main songwriters, Jones felt left out in the cold. He found solace in whiskey, marijuana, pills, and, beginning in 1965, plenty of acid.

Jones was the first Stone to take up with model Anita Pallenberg. Pallenberg remembers Jones' low tolerance level to hallucinogens; she says he would cower in a corner, describing the monsters and armies of black beetles he saw. Little by little, Jones' tenuous grip on sanity began to loosen.

In 1967, Jones, Pallenberg, fellow Stone Richards, and some other friends

took a trip to Morocco. Jones and Pallenberg fought bitterly, occasionally coming to blows. After a few days, Richards had seen enough. One afternoon, while Jones was out shopping, Richards spirited Pallenberg back to London. The two became lovers, and Brian was devastated. Jones' father blames the trauma brought on by this desertion for his son's downfall: "...when he lost the only girl he ever loved, this was a severe blow to him...that was the turning point in Brian's life."

Jones' instability began to affect his work, and the Stones weren't happy about it. In spring 1969, he was asked to leave the band. At about the same time, Jones bought a huge estate that had belonged to *Winnie-the-Pooh* author A. A. Milne. He loved the elegant mansion and decorated it in high style, with Moroccan flourishes. But the home also made a perfect setting for his consuming paranoia; he would occasionally call friends in London and whisper that he was being held there against his will by the hired help.

On the night of July 3, 1969, Jones consumed copious amounts of wine, vodka, and brandy, along with a few

The site of Brian Jones' drowning, the pool at his Sussex estate.

Rock and Roll REVEALED

AND THE BEAT [DOESN'T GO] ON?

Drummer Trouble

Rick Allen (Def Leppard): Lost an arm

Ginger Baker: Found guilty of tax evasion

Pete Best: Fired from the Beatles just before the band became famous

John Bonham: Overdose

Karen Carpenter: Died of complications from anorexia nervosa

Keith Moon: Overdose

Billy Murcia (New York Dolls): Overdose

Teddy Pendergrass (started out as a drummer): Paralyzed in a car crash

Jeff Porcaro (Toto): Died of a heart attack after spraying pesticides in his garden

Tommy Ramone: Replaced by Marky Ramone

Gina Schock: Heart surgery

All drummers for **Spinal Tap:** Died of various causes

Ringo Starr: Recovering alcoholic

Max Weinberg (E Street Band): Hand trouble

Dennis Wilson: Drowned

*M*embers of Spinal Tap, sans exploding drummer.

barbiturates. He and some friends went for a midnight swim. He wanted to stay in a little longer than the others; when they checked on him twenty minutes later, he was floating facedown. The autopsy revealed a fatty degeneration of the heart and liver, evidence of bronchial trouble, and of course, the residue of chronic drug abuse. (Jim Morrison also died on July 3, but two years later. Both musicians were also found dead in the water.)

As is usual in cases like this, rumors flew regarding the cause of death. They ranged from murder to suicide, and implicated the housekeeper, Keith Richards, and even the Mafia. But the most likely culprit was generally thought to be a combination of alcohol, drugs, and inescapable self-loathing. As rock writer

Greil Marcus later wrote about Jones: "You can't come down from being a Rolling Stone. No way down, and one way out."

Dennis Wilson was the only Beach Boy who knew how to surf. But on December 28, 1983, he was in no condition to catch a wave.

Dennis became a millionaire at sixteen, performing with brothers Carl and Brian. He was the sex symbol of the band, a sixties swinger, making music and breaking hearts. And he was certainly no stranger to the drug scene; according to one friend, "whatever he did, he did in excess."

By the early eighties, after four divorces, the Golden Boy was well on his way to becoming a rock and roll statistic. He had kicked heroin, but did a lot

of coke, washing it down with booze from a jug that never left his side. On that December day in 1983 he was drinking heavily, hanging out on a boat docked in a Marina Del Rey, California, slip with three friends. By late afternoon, he had finished off a fifth of vodka and some wine, and was bent on diving for treasure. His friends said there was no stopping him. Wilson made several dives, bringing up bits and pieces from the ocean floor. But after one dive, he didn't return. A friend called out to him, suspecting Dennis was, typically, playing a game, hiding under the dock. But it was no game. His friends hailed the passing harbor patrol and, thirty minutes later, Wilson's lifeless body was pulled from the bay. The endless summer was over.

I Don't Like Mondays

MURDERS

Sam Cooke's polished image and distinctive phrasing was a model for sixties soul singers.

Not all rock and roll deaths have been accidental; a handful of great voices have been silenced by a bullet.

One of the most shocking incidents was the shooting death of suave soulman Sam Cooke. In the early sixties, Cooke was a frequent chart-topper with hits like "You Send Me," and "Twistin' the Night Away." But in December 1964, the sophisticated stylist's life came to a shabby end at a cheap Los Angeles motel.

On the night of December 10, Cooke had picked up a young woman at a party. The woman claimed that she had expected to be driven home, but that Cooke (who was married at the time) took her to a motel, forced her into a room, and "began to rip [her] clothes off." When Cooke went into the bathroom, the woman escaped with most of her clothes and went to a phone booth on the motel lot to call for help. Cooke was furious and, clad only in a sports jacket and a pair of shoes, went looking for her. He stormed into the motel manager's office and demanded that she tell him the whereabouts of the woman. A struggle then ensued between Cooke and the manager, and in the midst of the fight, the manager was able to get her hands on a .22, which she used to shoot Cooke three times. At the trial, the manager maintained that Cooke continued to lunge after her, but she dodged him and proceeded to beat the flailing singer to death with a stick.

More tragic even than self-defensive murder is cold-blooded assassination. On October 23, 1980, Mark David Chapman signed himself out from work at a condominium in Hawaii as John Lennon. A month and a half later, on December 8, the troubled drifter confronted the real Lennon outside Lennon's apartment building in New York City with a gun.

The doorman, Jay Hastings, heard gunshots outside his office a few minutes before 11 P.M. Moments later, John Lennon stumbled in, clutching a stack of cassette tapes, a heartbreaking look of bewilderment on his face. His wife, Yoko Ono, hurried in after him, screaming, "John's been shot! John's been shot!" At first Hastings thought the events were some kind of terrible joke—until Lennon slumped to the floor. Hastings promptly rang the police alarm, then rushed to Lennon's side. Blood flowed from the great musician's mouth and chest.

When police arrived, they collared Chapman, who stood calmly outside, reading J.D. Salinger's book *The Catcher in the Rye*. Later, Chapman said the novel had inspired him to murder Lennon. Minutes later, at 11:07, Lennon was pronounced dead at Roosevelt Hospital.

Obviously, the reasons behind the act of an insane man are complex. Perhaps Chapman himself explained it best when he told a minister, not long after the murder, "I've been going through a torment for the last two or three months. It's a struggle between good and evil and right and wrong...I just gave in."

Equally sad and bizarre is the case of Marvin Gaye. During the course of his career, Gaye had enjoyed outstanding success, recording twenty-six albums and reaping the rewards of forty hit songs. His popularity dwindled a bit in the late seventies, but in 1982 he was topping the charts with his comeback smash hit, "Sexual Healing." Although his career seemed to be on the upswing, Gaye's personal life was a shambles. He was addicted to cocaine.

Allegedly, Gaye had been abused and battered as a child by his father, preacher Marvin Gay, Sr. (The singer had added an *e* to the family name.) Gaye had married twice; both of his stormy marriages had ended in divorce.

By 1983, Gaye's cocaine problem was so bad that he couldn't function on his own and was prone to very irrational behavior. He moved back into his parents' Los Angeles home, and once he did, completely succumbed to constant cocaine-induced paranoia that required him to keep a large arsenal of guns on hand. "He was turning into a monster," reveals his mother, Alberta Gay. "They [friends] kept coming by and giving him drugs. 'They won't stay away,' Marvin said. 'Just throw the drugs in the toilet, son,' I pleaded with him. But he didn't have the willpower. He just stayed in that room, looking at that gun. Guns were always on his mind." Gaye's sister Irene said that Gaye had "gone completely crazy. He couldn't even put on his clothes...."

Unfortunately, Gaye's father was as dependent on vodka as Marvin Jr. was on coke. The atmosphere in the house was sour and threatening, and on the morning of April 1, 1984, Marvin Sr. was in a particularly foul mood; he couldn't find a letter concerning an insurance matter. He charged into Marvin Jr.'s bedroom, where Alberta was attending to her son. Witnesses claim that Marvin Jr. was enraged by the intrusion; he pushed his father into the hall and began punching him. Alberta managed to separate the two men, and Marvin Jr. returned to his bedroom. A few moments later, though, Marvin Sr. appeared in the doorway holding a .38-caliber revolver. He shot his son in the chest. When Marvin fell to the ground, the ex-preacher aimed and fired again, at point-blank range. The brutal conflict was over—Marvin Jr. was dead. Once again, the golden voice of a troubled poet was stilled.

Above: Marvin Gaye in a mellow moment. Left: Legions of fans in New York City mourn the tragic death of John Lennon, 1980.

Chapter Four

Addicted to Love

Love's got nothing to do
with it: Tina Turner's sexy
moves have made her a
rock and roll idol as well
as a role model for many
of her contemporaries.

Rock and Roll REVEALED

Rock and roll has come a long way from the Beatles' innocent request, "I Want to Hold Your Hand," to George Michael's lusty demand, "I Want Your Sex." Ed Sullivan's insistence on shielding viewers from Elvis' gyrating hips seems quaint in the era of MTV orgies.

In the chaste social climate of the fifties, Elvis' manager, Colonel Tom Parker, felt compelled to disguise his marketing stratagem, coyly maintaining, "If I'd thought [Elvis] was doing it on purpose I'd have been against it; but he honestly just gets overexcited when he sings." The King himself was more forthright about the connection between sex and pop music: "[If] you take the wiggle out of it, it is finished."

Rock Dionysus David Lee Roth believes that performers with natural sex appeal are more likely to become successful. Roth speaks from experience: "I feel sexy a whole lot of the time. That's one of the reasons I'm in this job: to exercise my sexual fantasies. When I'm onstage, it's like doing it with 20,000 of your closest friends."

Mick Jagger has admitted that his stage show is entirely based on sexual attraction. "I entice the audience. I do it every way I can think of." Some audience members are more enticed than others; but ever since Bill Haley, young girls have lined up to give themselves, body and soul, to their favorite rockers.

Rock stars are almost always looking for those willing young girls—and that's where the roadies come in. Part of a roadie's job is to scan audiences for attractive women, then hand them backstage passes—the hope being that the women will ultimately entertain the troops. But the true warriors of groupiedom don't wait for an invitation. In his book, *Stone Alone*, Bill Wyman recounts that when the Stones entered hotel rooms, they routinely had to flush girls out of shower stalls and closets. Often the girls had reached their destination by performing various oral maneuvers on security guards.

Wyman recalls one episode in which he got to chatting with three fans in a hotel who were primed for a ménage à quatre with their favorite bassist. But just as things got rolling between the sheets, the other band members knocked on the door. They had heard about the group scene and wanted a piece of the action. Wyman told them to get lost, but they eventually persuaded a hotel porter to let them in. The girls were overwhelmed and quickly left. Wyman sulked, "They spoiled what might have been something special."

In 1965, Wyman estimated that during the band's first two years of existence, he had slept with 278 girls, Brian Jones 130, Mick Jagger 30, Keith Richards 6, and Charlie Watts—the faithful married man—none. Despite Jagger's provocative onstage leering, he was relatively faithful to girlfriend Chrissie Shrimpton back home, at least when compared to Wyman and Jones. Wyman and Jones, for their part, continued to be the most sexually promiscuous members of the band. But they paid the price, as they were slapped with multiple paternity suits.

The primary victims of groupie voracity are musicians' wives and girlfriends. Rod Stewart's former significant other, Britt Ekland, recalls a young blonde forcing her way into the couple's hotel room during a United States tour. "Where's Rod?" said the girl, "I'm going to screw him." Another time Britt received a letter from a groupie asking her to draw in detail a specific component of Rod's anatomy for her.

Todd Rundgren's longtime girlfriend Bebe Buell learned to get wise to groupies' tricks. When a group comes to town, she claims, groupies work like a tightly drilled platoon. For instance, two will befriend their idol's wife or girlfriend, leading her off on a shopping junket while another two go to work on her husband or boyfriend. Ron Wood's wife, Jo, says the best answer is to truly befriend groupies and try not to get riled; when a wife fights with her

husband over an admiring female, the marriage is weakened and the groupie scores a win.

The most notorious groupie of all is Pamela Des Barres, author of *I'm With the Band.* "Miss Pamela," as she was called, was in the top groupie echelon—quasiserious girlfriend to some of the hottest rockers—in the late sixties and early seventies. She reveled in her status, and on one occasion, perched on Jimmy Page's amplifier during a Led Zeppelin concert and preened as "the wild-eyed girls looked up at me and wondered which member of the group I was sleeping with...I was so proud."

Miss Pamela knew her romance with Page was something special when

Opposite: David Lee Roth has said that rock should give the "same kick as the first seven minutes of a porno flick."

WHEN THE WHIP COMES DOWN

Alleged Kinky Diversions

Chuck Berry: Likes to (secretly) videotape women in bathrooms

Brian Jones and Anita Pallenberg: Whips

Little Richard: Used to like to watch others have sex (including, on one occasion, his girlfriend and Buddy Holly)

Madonna: Spanking

Keith Moon: Liked to play roles with his bed partners, like the Schoolgirl and the Priest

John Phillips (formerly of the Mamas and the Papas): Spanking, tying women to bedposts, using whipped cream in a variety of ways

Elvis Presley: Women in white cotton underpants

Prince: Unwinds by lapping honey from the navels of models

Rod Stewart: Likes to wear women's underwear

Groupie high priestess Pamela Des Barres said of her first sexual encounter with Mick Jagger, "My nerves flew out the window as he threw me onto the mattress and turned me into a cheating trollop. It was fantastic."

he abated his sadistic tendencies for the duration of their affair, casting aside his whips as proof of his love. "All he did was chew me and slap me a little," Pamela notes. The only time she feared Page's wrath was when she worried that he might notice a hickey Mick Jagger had given her on her upper thigh. Apparently, the bruise went unnoticed.

But Pamela's high jinks were tame compared to the exploits of Chicago's legendary groupies, the Plaster Casters. The Casters had devised a unique entry into the Groupie Hall of Fame: they actually created plaster casts of famous rock and roll hard-ons. The process involved dipping the erect member into a gooey white substance, alginate, then

withdrawing it and filling the resulting hole with plaster, and an hour later: voilà! a perfect replica. Rockers from Jimi Hendrix to members of Led Zeppelin, the Animals, and Jefferson Airplane all chose to be thusly immortalized.

But groupies aren't the only ones who trade sexual favors for prestige. Just as in Hollywood lore, many rock stars have risen to the top by way of the bedroom.

Madonna is perhaps the most public sexual manipulator. The woman who considered the loss of her virginity "a career move" is unapologetically frank about her talents: "Manipulating people, that's what I'm good at."

When Madonna Ciccone moved from Michigan to New York City in 1978 to pursue a dance career, life was not a cabaret. She worked at a Dunkin' Donuts and lived amidst cockroaches and winos in a grungy neighborhood on the Lower East Side's East Fourth Street, between Avenues A and B. Finally, Madonna happened upon musician Dan Gilroy at a party and moved camp to his place in Queens. From Gilroy, Madonna picked up as much as she needed to know about musicianship to get started on a new path. She was a fast learner, and was soon gigging around town with her first band, Breakfast Club. When the band's achievements didn't match her aspirations, Madonna simply moved onward and upward. As for Mr. Gilroy, he had served his function as music teacher, and was no longer needed.

The Material Girl was not above pulling the strings of both sexes to get ahead. When she realized that successful band manager Camille Barbone (a bisexual) could help her, Madonna wasted no time working on her. "She seduced me psychologically," says Barbone. "After that, I put her first, which was my downfall." Barbone hired topnotch studio musicians to back Madonna in her new band, Emmy.

The band recorded some songs, and Madonna took the tape to various

dance clubs, where she was already getting noticed for her uninhibited moves and provocative, belly-baring outfits. She charmed Danceteria DJ Mark Kamins into introducing her to record label executives by promising him that he could produce her first album. But when Sire Records signed Madonna for that album, the Boy Toy promptly dumped Kamins like a hot potato.

Next on old Madonna's hit list was DJ-producer Jellybean Benitez, who introduced her to the right people and helped define the "Madonna sound" on her first hit album. Benitez slaved away at remixing "Holiday," the dance hit that ultimately catapulted Madonna into the limelight. And once she was there, she could have her pick of producers. Exit Jellybean.

When Madonna wanted to turn her attentions to the silver screen, Sean Penn and Warren Beatty were happy to help. Ironically, on their first date, Penn took Madonna to a party at Beatty's house. The romance between Penn and Madonna blossomed into true love, marriage, and added Hollywood cachet for Madonna. Though her only film collaboration with her husband was the disastrous *Shanghai Surprise*, marriage to Penn was an entrance into the inner circle of A-list movie making.

When their stormy marriage dissolved, Madonna found herself a more powerful, press-friendly playmate in notorious ladykiller Beatty. This high-watt liaison made excellent publicity for the pair's costarring turn in Beatty's *Dick Tracy*. By this time, despite frequent critical drubbing, Madonna had a solid foothold in Hollywood. The cooling of Beatty's ardor was no threat to Madonna's career; the star now had what she wanted—the clout to go it alone in movies, sans Svengali.

Bette Midler once introduced Madonna as the girl who "pulled herself up by her own bra straps." So far in the nineties, Madonna seems content to make her own luck, instead of romancing her way to the top. But her days of

sexual manipulation are far from over: 1992 ended with the triple whammy of the completion of the steamy film *Body of Evidence*, the release of the album *Erotica*, and the publishing event of the year, the photography book *Sex*. The latter entry was Madonna-hype at its best: a selection of quasipornographic shots of the star in various compromising poses, packaged like plutonium and guarded like the crown jewels. Although many critics found the photographs no more artful or provocative than standard porno fare, the book was a runaway hit, selling a half million copies in the United States alone in its first week of publication. Yes, pop culture's great puppeteer had struck again.

Perhaps the opposite side of Madonna's sexual coin is her friend Prince. Rather than sleeping his way up the ladder of success, the pride of Minneapolis has made a hobby out of

molding the careers of his bedmates, whose numbers include performers Vanity, Apollonia, and Sheena Easton. And rather than jealously resenting the star's revolving door of protégées, all of Prince's former lovers gush with affection for him. Says Apollonia, who starred in Prince's film *Purple Rain*, "I will love Prince until the day I die." Enthuses former musical collaborator Vanity, "He's the most romantic man I've ever met in my life." And during their short romance, Sheena Easton, the lissome Scot for whom Prince wrote the hit songs "Sugar Walls" and "Eternity," swooned, "The happiest times I've ever had in my life are when I'm with Prince. He's the only one who can give me everything I need—friendship, understanding, creative stimulation, and most of all, love."

In a world in which many male rockers view women as a kind of fashion accessory, Prince appears to be...a prince. Vanity has been quoted as saying that the singer was the best lover she'd ever had. And in rock and roll, it's the great seducers who triumph.

Above: Prince (with percussionist Sheila E.) molds princesses out of raw talent. Left: Media darlings Warren Beatty and Madonna rehearsed their Dick Tracy love scenes extensively off-camera. Madonna embarrassed the normally reticent Beatty by detailing their sex life for the press.

Love Stinks

ROCK AND ROLL ROMANCES

Jerry Lee Lewis rarely spent evenings at home alone with teen bride Myra. Recounts Myra, "He usually arrived unannounced in the middle of the night, wanting a hot meal and hot sex."

Not all rock and roll relationships are strictly carnal; sometimes Cupid's arrow pierces through skintight leather. Many musicians do sign up for Happily Ever After, but when the fairy tale goes sour—often amid drugs, deception, and depravity—the results can be quite devastating.

One of the most notorious rock and roll husbands is piano-thumper Jerry Lee "the Killer" Lewis. In 1957, the pride of Ferriday, Louisiana, was a prime candidate to usurp the throne of King Elvis with hits like "Great Balls of Fire" and "Whole Lotta Shakin' Going On." Then

the news came out: Lewis had secretly married his thirteen-year-old cousin, Myra. When she left home, Myra didn't have a suitcase, so she packed her things in a red cardboard dollhouse that she'd received for Christmas. When news of the marriage broke during Lewis' British tour, the Killer goofily tried to soothe shocked fans by claiming that Myra was fifteen, instead of thirteen. To further complicate matters, word came out that Lewis had never gotten around to divorcing his two previous wives. He had left his second wife when she bore him a dark-haired son; Jerry Lee believed a genuine offspring would have inherited his trademark golden locks.

Lewis' marriage to Myra ended in divorce thirteen years later in 1970, with Myra telling tales of Lewis beating her up in full view of their daughter.

His next marriage—in 1971, to Jaren Gunn—officially lasted two

weeks. In fourteen days, Jaren had her fill of Lewis' "cruel and inhuman treatment, adultery, habitual drunkenness, and habitual use of drugs." The couple separated and eight years (and one child) later, Jaren finally sued for divorce. According to a 1984 *Rolling Stone* magazine report by Richard Ben Cramer, the Killer made a chilling comment when Jaren asked him about child support: "You are not going to be around very long anyway, and if you don't get off my back and leave me alone, you will end up in the bottom of the lake...."

In fact, Jaren ended up at the bottom of a swimming pool just before her settlement came through. The mysterious death was ruled an accident.

Lewis' fifth trip down the aisle, in 1983, with twenty-five-year-old Shawn Stephens, proved the most infamous of all. The young, vivacious former cocktail waitress thought she had realized her dreams of glamour and luxury by marrying Lewis, but the dream immediately became a nightmare. The wedding ceremony took place on the patio of Lewis' Nesbit, Mississippi, mansion. The nuptials seemed to indicate a pleasant May-December union, but the day after the event was ominous.

According to Shawn's sister Shelley, Shelley went into the Lewises' kitchen for a couple of beers, where she was confronted by an angry Jerry Lee, who asked her what she wanted. "He started pounding his fist on the counter, screaming, 'You scared of me? You should be. Why do you think they call me the Killer? How'd I get that name, huh?' Then he slapped my face." Later that day she saw Jerry hit Shawn. Shelley was furious and wanted to call the police. But, according to Shelley, "Shawn said it wouldn't be a good idea to go to the police down there, because they were with Jerry." Later still, Shelley saw Lewis knock Shawn clear across the living room. Shawn subsequently threatened to leave him. Shelley claims Jerry Lee responded, "You're my wife. I'll kill you before you leave me."

Two and a half months after the wedding, in August 1983, Shawn was found dead in an upstairs bedroom of Lewis' house. It has never been determined who called the ambulance, but one of the ambulance attendants said that when he arrived on the scene, he observed that Lewis' speech was heavily slurred and his bathrobe was stained with blood. There also was blood under Shawn's fingernails, in her hair, and on her clothes. One of the attendants noticed that one of Shawn's arms had several horrible bruises on it, as if someone had grabbed her and tugged hard, and her neck was discolored. None of this appeared on the official report.

When local deputy sheriff Jack McCauley arrived, Lewis took him into his den for a long, private discussion. McCauley has never publicly revealed what the two talked about; he didn't even file a report on the conversation. It's possible that the fact that Lewis had been the largest contributor to the campaign of the sheriff-elect influenced the deputy. The sheriff hired Dr. Jerry Francisco, the man who had maintained that Elvis Presley died of heart failure, to perform the autopsy. Francisco was expensive, but Lewis offered to pay his fee. The final verdict was an overdose of methadone; there was "no indication at all of foul play."

The morticians, John and Danny Phillips, were a father-and-son team. When Danny Phillips released a description of Shawn's bruised body, his father warned him about their "stake in the community." In his interview with Cramer, Danny Phillips said, "I'd never say Jerry Lee killed that girl...but I'd like to see it investigated. To me, I just can't believe that girl got to that bed and lay down and died. You just can't make me believe it."

Nevertheless, Lewis' fifth wife was dead and, as Lewis' road manager J.W. Whitten bragged to Cramer, "They'll never bust [Jerry Lee] in De Soto County. That's like bustin' Elvis in Memphis. Never. Never."

With his matrimonial track record, you'd think Lewis might opt for bachelorhood. But no. In April 1984, Lewis tied the knot for a sixth time, with then-twenty-one-year-old country singer Kerrie Lynn McCarver. Three years later, the union produced an heir: Jerry Lee Lewis III (Lewis' son by Myra, Jerry Lee, Jr., was killed in an auto accident in 1973.) Will domesticity calm the Killer instinct? It remains to be seen.

Jerry Lee Lewis is certainly not the only violent husband in rock and roll. James Brown has reportedly been beating wives and girlfriends for thirty years. In spring 1988, Brown began a violent spree by systematically shooting all of his wife Adrienne's clothes—including two expensive fur coats—full of holes. Brown was eventually arrested, after firing several rounds at a car Adrienne

Below, left: Jerry Lee and his fifth wife, Shawn Stevens Lewis, at a Grammy Awards party in Los Angeles five months before the young woman's mysterious death. Below, right: Six is a charm: "The Killer" with his sixth wife, Kerrie, and their young son.

GOING TO THE CHAPEL

Unusual Weddings

Jon and Dorothea Bon Jovi: The bride and groom both wore black leather for their wedding in front of the Graceland wedding chapel in Las Vegas.

David and Angie Bowie: One of their witnesses was a woman the couple had slept with the night before. The Bowies proceeded to conduct an "open" bisexual marriage.

Mick and Bianca Jagger: The in-crowd giggled over how much the bride resembled the groom. One onlooker commented on how happy the vain Stones frontman must be, now that he can "make love to himself."

Madonna and Sean Penn: The wedding started with a bang, that is, Penn shooting at intruding press helicopters with a .45. Madonna wore a strapless tulle gown and a black bowler with a veil. The noise from the choppers was deafening.

Jim Morrison and Patricia Kennealy: The wedding was a black magic affair held in Kennealy's apartment on the evening of the summer solstice in 1969. The couple wore black robes and united by nicking their wrists and mingling blood.

Rod Stewart and Rachel Hunter: During the ceremony, Rachel Stewart pinched Rod's behind for the entertainment of the wedding guests, who broke into spontaneous applause.

Sting and Trudie Styler: The couple wore $250,000 worth of Versace. Sting serenaded her with "Someone to Watch Over Me." They and 245 close friends dined on filet of bass, fresh baby vegetables, and crème brûlée.

Frank and Gail Zappa: In lieu of a ring, Frank gave Gail a ballpoint pen that said "Congratulations from Mayor Lindsay," which he pinned to her dress during the ceremony.

Opposite: "After all, we've already got the house and kids...:" Sting and longtime live-in, Trudie Styler, tie the knot in a fairy-tale wedding. Left: Elvis and Priscilla married in secret at a Las Vegas hotel but had a second reception at Graceland for Memphis friends.

was driving and beating her with a metal mop handle. Although he got off with a fine for the offense, later that year Brown was sentenced to six years in prison for driving under the influence of PCP and attempting to elude police (see page 47.)

Compared to Brown and Lewis, Elvis Presley was an angel. In 1959, Elvis fans waved a tearful good-bye as their handsome idol was inducted into the United States Army. Presley was assigned to Wiesbaden, Germany, where he met Priscilla Beaulieu, the fourteen-year-old daughter of an army captain. Priscilla remembers the embarrassment of that first meeting, when Presley laughed at her admission that she was in the ninth grade. "Why, you're just a baby," he said.

Baby or no, Presley was hooked, and the two began spending a lot of time together. Priscilla's first kiss was with the hottest sex symbol in the world. Her parents were skeptical and insisted on strict dating rules, but the

lovebirds worked around it. The couple spent many passionate hours in Presley's bedroom—he lived off-base—but he did not want to consummate their affair. "Someday we will," Priscilla said he'd say to her, "...but not now. You're just too young."

According to Priscilla, Presley told her she fit his idea of the perfect woman: a soft-spoken brunette with blue eyes. "He wanted to mold me to his opinions and preferences," said Priscilla, "...I wore the clothes, hairstyle and makeup of his careful choosing." When Presley's tour of duty was over, Priscilla was heartbroken, fearing she'd never see him again. But two years after he left Germany, he begged Priscilla's parents to let her finish her senior year of high school in Memphis, hinting that he intended to marry her one day. Priscilla's parents agreed to the proposition under the provision that Priscilla move in with Presley's parents, rather than with him at Graceland. Everyone agreed, and Priscilla headed

for Vernon and Gladys Presley's home in Memphis. By the end of her senior year, however, Priscilla had taken up residence in Graceland.

Elvis and Priscilla finally married in 1967, but did not live happily ever after. As Priscilla notes in her autobiography, *Elvis and Me*, Presley had once told her that he'd never been able to have sex with a woman who'd had a child. Indeed, as soon as Priscilla became pregnant, the King's eye began to wander. Priscilla was devastated by rumors of an affair with Nancy Sinatra, and the road grew even rockier after the birth of their only child, daughter Lisa Marie. According to Priscilla, the couple's sexual activity became negligible, and Elvis began spending more and more time on the road.

To fill her days and release frustrations, Priscilla studied music, dance, and martial arts. The King's young wife eventually found solace in the arms of karate instructor Mike Stone. In 1972 Priscilla moved out of the Presley's Los

Rock and Roll REVEALED

Angeles home; in 1973 Elvis filed for divorce. Although Elvis had carried on his own affairs without much discretion, perhaps most notably with actress Cybill Shepherd, he was truly crushed by Priscilla's infidelity. He poured out his heart to a friend: "She has everything money can buy...cars, homes, an expense account. And she knows that all she has to do is ask, and I'll get her whatever she wants. I can't understand...I love that woman."

Elvis and Priscilla remained friends until Elvis' death, holding hands as they listened to the judge's explanation of the divorce proceedings. But Elvis had squandered true love, and ended up alone in the heartbreak hotel.

Elvis and Jerry Lee weren't the only rockers with a taste for teens; dating the underaged is a time-honored tradition in current music circles, too. A present-day champion of cradle robbing is Rolling Stone Bill Wyman. In 1984, the bassist spotted a young girl dancing at the British Rock Awards. As Wyman tells it, "...my heart just jumped. She took my breath away. I felt like I'd been whacked over the head with a hammer. I immediately said...'I've got to meet that girl, got to talk to her.'"

The girl and her older sister were brought over. The older girl turned out to be fifteen, and Wyman's object of affection, Mandy Smith, was thirteen. The sisters expressed an interest in modeling; Wyman offered to set them up with a friend who owned an agency in order to spark Mandy's interest.

At the modeling agency, both girls were told they were too young. But Wyman obviously didn't think so: he was already in hot pursuit, visiting the Smith house, bearing the traditional chocolates and flowers. On one occasion, Bill cornered Mandy in the hallway and grabbed her for a kiss. Wyman wrote of the experience: "She was a woman at thirteen, and certainly looked like the twenty-year-old I had originally believed her to have been. When I asked her mother if I could take Mandy

out to dinner, I was told she had been going to clubs and pubs for a year and a half; there was no objection."

The two started to date and—despite his friends' warnings—Wyman fell deeply in love. But because of her age, Wyman was afraid to take Mandy out in public. He continued to squire other women to keep up appearances, which led to rifts between the two. They broke up on Mandy's sixteenth birthday, and Bill was heartbroken.

After the split, Mandy innocently mentioned her friendship with Wyman to a group at a party, one of whom was a reporter. The next day, the tabloids screamed of cradle robbing. Wyman was horrified because he felt he had taken care of Mandy and "treated her honorably." He maintained that he had tried to help her and educate her. He said he "simply wanted to be with her."

Eventually the fiasco quieted down, and Wyman was never charged with any wrongdoing. But after a two-year separation, the lovers started seeing each other again. This time, all the innuendo in the world couldn't stop true love. The two were married a year later, in June 1990, thirty-four-year age difference be damned (although guests couldn't help but notice that the then-fifty-two-year-old Wyman was wearing quite a bit of makeup.) Said the gallant bridegroom, "I hope this is forever. I just tore up my address book." One of the wedding presents was a walker "to help Bill get through the honeymoon."

However, the marriage quickly went sour, for Mandy insisted her mother accompany the newlyweds on their honeymoon. By the end of the year, the marriage was dying. Apparently, Stones drummer Charlie Watts had hit the mark with his dark wedding day comment, "I wish Bill all the best, but I've never said this would be a good match."

Certainly, love at first sight can be deceptive. But when that first sight is of one of the most beautiful women in the world, common sense often goes out the window. That is why so many rock

stars pair up with models. After all, rock and roll and modeling have a lot in common—high visibility, lots of eyeliner, teased-to-death hair, and pouty poses. And in the age of video, the twain are more likely than ever to meet on soundstages (Ric Ocasek and supermodel wife Paulina Porizkova are just one example). As for the psychological aspects of a rocker choosing a model, rock writer Jon Pareles notes, "It's not much of a stretch from wearing the fanciest leather jacket or driving the flashiest car to squiring the cover girl of the month—they all prove that the boy has arrived. And if rockers are living out their fans' fantasy lives by remaining in a state of extended adolescence, what could be more ego-satisfying than dating the adult equivalent of a homecoming queen?" Ego-satisfying, maybe, but not always easy. The union of two pampered media darlings is not always so congenial once the lights and cameras are turned off.

Rocker-Model Couples

David Bowie and Iman

Eric and Pattie Boyd Harrison Clapton

Eric Clapton and Carla Bruni

Elvis Costello and Bebe Buell

Bob Dylan and Edie Sedgwick

Bryan Ferry and Jerry Hall

Michael Hutchence and Helena Christiansen

Michael Hutchence and Elle MacPherson

Mick Jagger and Jerry Hall

Mick Jagger and Chrissie Shrimpton

Brian Jones and Anita Pallenberg

Billy Joel and Christie Brinkley

Simon LeBon and Yasmin

Madonna and Tony Ward

John Mellencamp and Elaine Irwin

John Oates and Nancy Hunter

Ric Ocasek and Paulina Porizkova

Keith Richards and Patti Hansen

Keith Richards and Anita Pallenberg

Axl Rose and Stephanie Seymour

Todd Rundgren and Bebe Buell

Bruce Springsteen and Julianne Phillips

Ringo Starr and Barbara Bach

Rod Stewart and Bebe Buell

Rod Stewart and Kelly Emberg

Rod Stewart and Rachel Hunter

Roger Taylor and Renée Simonsen

Alex Van Halen and Kelly Carter

Ron Wood and Jo Howard

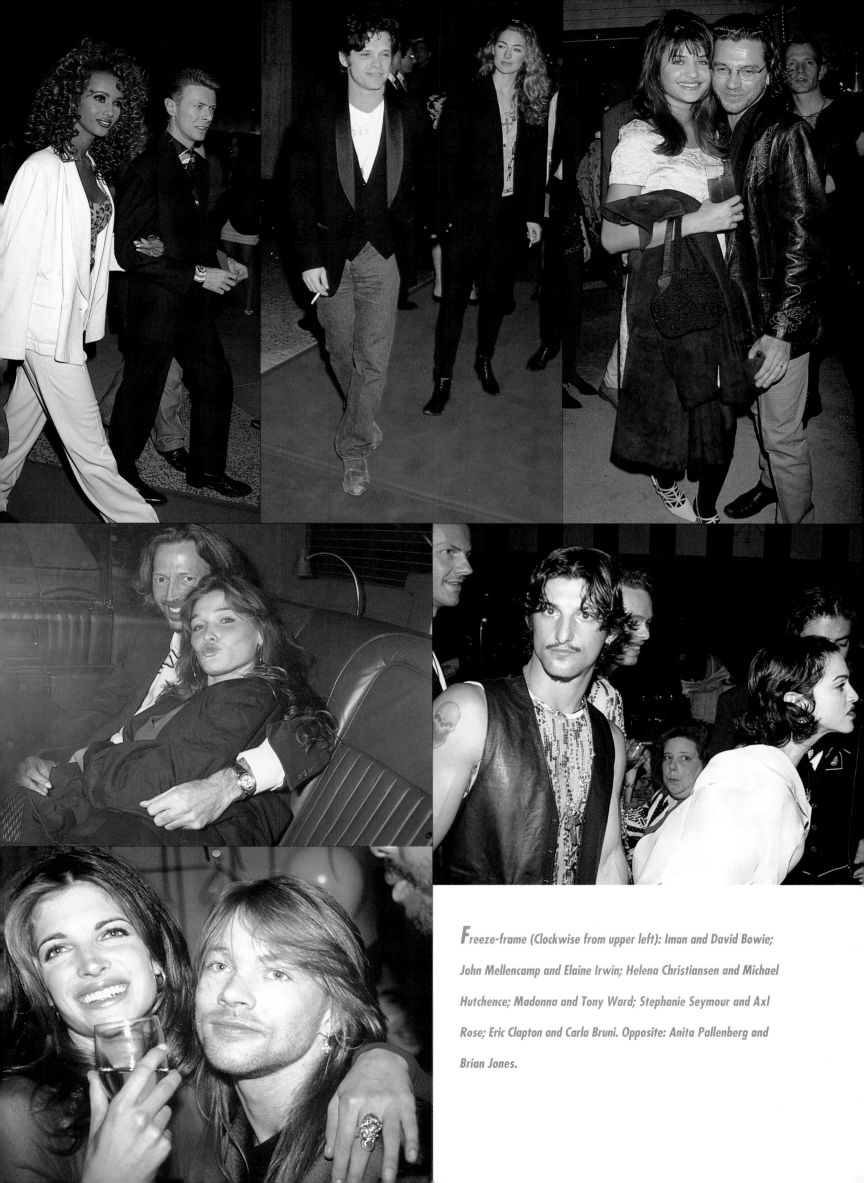

*F*reeze-frame (Clockwise from upper left): Iman and David Bowie; John Mellencamp and Elaine Irwin; Helena Christiansen and Michael Hutchence; Madonna and Tony Ward; Stephanie Seymour and Axl Rose; Eric Clapton and Carla Bruni. Opposite: Anita Pallenberg and Brian Jones.

One of the most romantic—or shocking, depending on how you look at it—rock and roll love stories is that of Eric Clapton and actress-model Pattie Boyd Harrison Clapton. Clapton became friends with Beatle George Harrison in the late sixties, and the two collaborated on such songs as "Badge." But whenever Eric would spend time with George and his wife, Pattie, he would feel a pang of longing "...every time I left...I remember feeling a dreadful emptiness—because I was certain I was never going to meet a woman quite that beautiful for myself.... I knew I was in love...it got heavier and heavier for me."

Eric became obsessed with Pattie, and even briefly dated her sister as a substitute. In time Pattie, too, felt the tug of illicit attraction, and the two began an affair. Lovely Pattie was an inspiration for both her men; Harrison wrote the much-covered "Something" about her, and Clapton's "Layla" was a passionate bid for her affection.

In fact, Clapton was so desperate, he used emotional blackmail to try to get her to leave Harrison. Clapton showed her a packet of heroin and told her that if she didn't leave Harrison, he'd start taking the drug. Pattie retreated to her husband, and Clapton went into drug-abusing isolation for the next two years (see page 55). When Clapton reemerged, he sought out George and Pattie at a party; he confronted the Beatle and told him he was in love with Pattie. When Clapton asked Harrison what he was going to do about the situation, Clapton claims Harrison said, "'Whatever you like, man. It doesn't worry me.'" Clapton says that Harrison "was being very spiritual about it and saying everybody should do their own thing."

After such faint protest from her husband, Pattie left him and moved in with Clapton. Clapton and Pattie finally married in 1979, and weathered both stormy and blissful times before separating for good in the late eighties. Clapton has said that part of the problem in the relationship was stress over Pattie's inability to conceive. He resorted to impregnating other women—Italian actress Lory Del Santo and, allegedly, nightclub singer Alina Morini—and Mrs. Clapton did not take kindly to it. In April 1988, Pattie filed for divorce.

Perhaps the most infamous model-slayer on the scene is Rod Stewart. Rod is easily as famous for his ever-changing Stepford Girlfriends—all stunning leggy blondes—as he is for rasping hits like "Do Ya Think I'm Sexy?" The first Stewart pal (as in palimony) to step into the limelight with the Singing Scot was Swedish actress Britt Ekland. Ekland caught her first sight of Rod in the mid-seventies, when Joan Collins took her to his concert. Britt's first impression was...impressed: "I looked into the spotlight and there was this incredible man, so sexy, so animal-like."

The two were introduced after the gig and went on to a party at Cher's house. They quickly fell in love and began adding their golden-haired glamour to various Hollywood hot spots. Rod remembers going to a party at Joni Mitchell's house at which Bob Dylan and Paul McCartney started an impromptu jam session. When the superstars invited Rod to join them, he declined, preferring to be with Britt. Rod commented, "I don't think anyone has ever turned down the chance to jam with Bob Dylan, but I was so much in love with Britt."

Rock and Roll REVEALED

On Britt Ekland:
"I'm a changed man. I just don't fancy other birds anymore. Britt's everything I want."

On wife Alana Stewart:
"For the first time in my life I will be faithful to one woman—my wife...we were made for each other."

On Rachel Hunter, on his wedding day: "I feel like a dog with two dicks."

On Kelly Emberg: "She can trust me. I'm not the same person I was."

YOU'RE IN MY HEART

Rod Stewart in Love

Britt recalls, "Very soon we were making love three or four times a day. We were like two pieces of interlocking jigsaw.... Rod regarded every orgasm as a testimony of his love for me."

When Britt heard through the grapevine that Rod liked big-breasted women, she offered to have hers enlarged. Rod said no. According to Britt, "He thought I was perfect as I stood. He liked my teenage-preserved figure and my long blonde hair.... He liked me always to dress in virginal white stockings, panties, petticoat, negligée and peel it all off like the leaves of an artichoke...once, just for the kick of it, we made love on the backseat of my Mercedes, which we chose to park in the long, unlit drive of the house belonging to my neighbor Goldie Hawn—whom I'm sure would have been very understanding if she'd found out!"

Eventually, however, Rod's eye wandered, the pair split up, and in 1977 Britt slapped him with a $15 million palimony suit. For her troubles, she was awarded $500,000 in property.

Next Rod got serious with the ex-wife of ever-tan actor George Hamilton, Alana. She was Stewart's type: a tall beautiful blonde with legs from here to there and back again. The two quickly became inseparable, sometimes even stepping out in matching outfits. When they married in 1979, Rod's mother whispered in his ear, "Make sure you keep your trousers on in the future. Be a good boy."

Alana bore Rod two children—a boy and a girl—and for a time the couple happily played house in their Holmby Hills mansion. But soon Rod's adolescent demons began nagging at him. As he noted at the time, "It's very confusing.... Half of me is the family man and the other half is the thirty-five-year-old who will not grow up."

On one occasion, the specter of Stewart's former "true love" reared its head; allegedly Britt Ekland approached Rod at a party and climbed onto his lap, in full view of his wife. Alana cooled Ekland off by dumping a flute of champagne down the back of her dress.

Though both Rod and Alana tried hard to make a success of the marriage, the union was kaput by 1983. In an angry statement, Alana referred to Rod's return to philandering: "If he wants to go out with a series of mind-less moronic young models rather than being with me and the children, I don't think I'm losing anything.... He's lost a wife and two kids. All I've lost is someone who can't grow up."

In 1983, Rod hooked up with statuesque blonde model Kelly Emberg. Although Stewart was relatively faithful to Emberg, and she gave birth to their daughter, the pairing didn't last.

Enter model Rachel Hunter of New Zealand in 1990. Exit Emberg, waving $35 million worth of palimony papers. Hunter was not impressed with Stewart's initial plan of romantic attack: he followed her around a disco mimicking lines from her exercise video. But the old Stewart charm won out, and soon Rod and the fun-loving, tall, blonde, and—you guessed it, young—model from Down Under were head over heels in love. In autumn 1990, Rod and Rachel sent out wedding invitations that read: "Are you sitting down? Rachel Hunter and Rod Stewart invite you to be a guest at their wedding."

In 1992, Hunter gave birth to Stewart's fourth child, Renee. Will the Singing Scotsman bolt after the baby has arrived, as has been his pattern? Only time will tell. But Rod has this to say about his epitaph: "I am a musician. I'm not a sex machine. I know I've written some good songs which have made people happy. I would like to be remembered for that, not how many women I've bedded."

One of the most scrutinized rocker-model pairings of the eighties was that of Bruce "the Boss" Springsteen and Julianne Phillips. The two met backstage at one of his concerts and were married in a secret midnight ceremony in Julianne's hometown in 1985. Everything seemed rosy for a while, but Springsteen's 1987 album *Tunnel of*

In February 1988, public smiles masked a breakdown in Bruce and Julianne's tunnel of love.

Rock and Roll REVEALED

Love, a little heavy on the dirges about love gone sour, suggested that perhaps all was not so hot at home. On the "Tunnel of Love" tour in 1988, Bruce was photographed frolicking poolside with backup singer Patti Scialfa. When photos of the pair kissing in the streets of Rome hit newsstands, a shocked Julianne called her lawyer.

Springsteen had known Scialfa since the seventies, when both were familiar faces in the Asbury Park, New Jersey, club scene. In 1984, Scialfa joined Springsteen's band. A friend of Scialfa's claims that the redhead had had a crush on her Boss from the get-go, but that the two were just friends until 1988.

The rumor spread that the true cause of the bust-up was Phillips' pursuit of her acting career at a time when Springsteen wanted to start a family. Julianne denies this, claiming the couple had been trying to have a baby. Regardless, the couple divorced in 1989. Julianne received a healthy alimony settlement, on the condition that she refrain from penning a tell-all book.

Two years later, Springsteen wed Scialfa in a romantic candlelight ceremony in the backyard of the couple's Beverly Hills estate.

A friend of the Boss had this to say about Bruce's matrimonial track record: "With Julianne, [Bruce] was euphoric, but it wasn't real. The truth is, he and Julianne had nothing in common. Patti and Bruce, on the other hand, have everything in common."

So it would seem. Springsteen and Scialfa now have offspring Evan James and Jessica in common, and continue to collaborate on musical projects. In interviews, Springsteen seems content with domestic life; perhaps what he needed all along was the love of a Jersey girl.

On the European front, one would think that a cocky British "street-fighting man," and a willowy high-fashion Texan model would have little in common. But the union of Mick Jagger and Jerry Hall seemed remarkably sturdy—at least, until recently.

When Jagger and Hall met at a dinner party in 1977, Jagger was in the process of a nasty, and costly, divorce from his wife, Bianca. The seven-year marriage had been rife with reports of dalliances (see the chart on pages 92–93 for a more in-depth view of Jagger's love life) on both sides, and at first, Jerry might have seemed to be the flavor of the month. For her part, Hall was engaged to British retro crooner Bryan Ferry, of Roxy Music; in no time flat, she ditched Ferry and hooked up with Jagger. The two established something like a domestic life and seemed remarkably compatible. But Jerry longed for a stone—a diamond, for instance— from her Stone, and tried tactics from bedroom pyrotechnics to jealousy ploys to win a commitment from him. But Jagger's feelings on fidelity remained ambivalent. As he revealed in a 1986 *Ladies Home Journal* article, "I do need a stable relationship in my life, and you can't have a stable relationship and go around and sleep with everything in sight. However, I've also told Jerry that I can't feel cut off from one half of the population. You can't stop having affairs if they come along, but there is a difference between that and trying to be with every girl you meet."

Apparently, Mick's availability remained the same even after the couple finally wed in November 1990. By this time, Hall was probably used to the affairs but drew the line when Jagger became obsessed with Italian model-heiress Carla Bruni. The tabloids reported that the day after Jerry gave birth to the couple's third child, Georgia, Mick flew off to Thailand for a rendezvous with Bruni. (In interviews, Bruni has claimed to have only "met" Jagger and to have found his pursuit of her annoying.) Hall tried marriage counseling and even called Bruni and "told her to leave [her] man alone," but to no avail. As one friend commented: "There is no doubt that [Mick] loves Jerry and she loves him, but he has an insatiable desire for dabbling with other women—especially striking blondes under twenty-five." Jerry Hall shouldn't have been surprised by the Bruni affair; after all, it wasn't the first time Jagger had left a wife for a young, leggy blonde model.

Perhaps the most stormy rock and roll marriages have involved the union of two stars.

You could say John Phillips asked for it. When he started seeing seventeen-year-old Michelle Gilliam, he was still married to his first wife, Susie. But not for long. As Phillips relates in his autobiography, *Papa John*, scrappy young Michelle paid his wife a visit while he

was on the road. She introduced herself, then laid down the law, saying, "My name's Michelle Gilliam, but in a couple of years it's going to be Michelle Phillips. You might as well give up now. I love him, and he's going to be mine."

She was right. The two soon married, and, along with Dennis Doherty and Cass Elliott, formed the Mamas and the Papas.

Early on in the band's career, Michelle had an affair with the other Papa, Denny, causing considerable tension in the group. It also didn't help matters any that Mama Cass had a serious crush on Denny. As John said, "My dream of a peaceful 'family' of musical

artists was crumbling fast." Michelle came back to John, but as the group's star rose, both husband and wife played musical beds around Los Angeles. John recounts marital life in the swinging sixties: "I could never accuse Michelle of being devious. Just blunt and defiant. She would call me at home and interrupt herself by saying, 'What, Gene?' with her hand over the phone. 'Oh, anyway, John,' she would then continue, 'Gene and I are in bed, but before we go to sleep I wanted to ask you what time the Mamas are supposed to be at the studio tomorrow.'"

But in 1968, the band split up. Two years later, Phillips and Michelle

divorced, and Phillips embarked on a nightmarish odyssey into drug addiction (see page 57).

Tall, attractive folk rockers James Taylor and Carly Simon didn't play in the same band, but seemed kindred spirits nonetheless when they wed in 1972. At the time, Sweet Baby James was the headliner of the family, with Top Ten hits like "Fire and Rain," and "You've Got a Friend." But as Carly's runaway hit "You're So Vain" climbed to the top of the charts, the marriage began to slide.

Taylor had been battling a penchant for depression with drugs and alcohol for most of his adult life. At the age of twenty-two, with a hit record on the charts, Taylor was already a heroin addict. During their marriage, Taylor and Simon hung out with a wild, creative crowd that included John Belushi and party-hearty Jimmy Buffett. Parties raged long into the night and tended to get crazy; on one occasion, Taylor bit a hole in a friend's guitar. The couple's two young children, Ben and Sarah, found it difficult to understand their father's mood swings and frequent absences. For her part, Carly hated drugs and grew tired of trying to keep up with the coke-snorting jet set. In 1982, she sued for divorce.

Double the drug abuse and marital strains and you get another seventies phenomenon, Fleetwood Mac. Mac's lineup included couple John and Christine McVie and lovers Lindsey Buckingham and Stevie Nicks. By the time the band recorded *Rumours*, in 1976, both unions were on the rocks. On the last tour, Christine was secretly shacked up with the lighting director, and Stevie was half joking that Lindsey was more interested in his guitar than he was in her.

In his book on the band, *Fleetwood: My Life With Fleetwood Mac*, Mick Fleetwood—who was also separated from his wife at the time—describes the misery of working on an album about shattered relationships with the

four dueling exes trapped in one room. Anguished rumors were flying over who was seeing whom after recording hours, and nerves were further frayed by a blizzard of cocaine. John McVie remembers having a lump in his throat the entire time the group was arduously recording and overdubbing his wife's song of emancipation, "Don't Stop (Thinking About Tomorrow)." As Fleetwood remembers it, "the sound of breaking hearts filled the studio."

One star marriage that has bent without breaking—so far—is that of Valerie Bertinelli and Eddie Van Halen. The couple met backstage in 1980 at a Van Halen concert when then nineteen-year-old Bertinelli was still playing a lovable teen on the hit television series *One Day at a Time*. Valerie says she was attracted to Ed for his tender, emotional side. However, on the other side of that coin was a serious drinking problem. It took Valerie several years to realize what she had gotten herself into. As she told *Redbook* magazine in 1990, "I thought, 'Okay, so he gets drunk once in a while.' But the older I get, the more I think, 'This is boring. This isn't fun to live with anymore.' Sometimes I wonder why I stay. I have no regrets, though. I like my life. I like that I got married and settled down. I still love him."

Several years ago, Eddie and his brother, Alex, committed themselves to the Betty Ford Center. But Valerie believes Eddie went only because his brother was going; he wasn't yet truly ready to commit to changing his life. Ultimately, the treatment didn't stick, but Eddie tried again in another program in 1990 and seems to be doing much better.

Valerie herself goes regularly to Al-Anon—a program for friends and families of alcoholics—to try to learn to cope. When asked why she stays in such a painful marriage, Valerie responded frankly, "It isn't always painful. Ed doesn't beat me. He doesn't abuse me. He hurts himself. He's got a problem

I'm not happy with, but I bring stability to his life. And besides, I love him. It's my weakness. Some people are addicted to food; I'm addicted to my husband. I can't say that we're really great friends—we don't have a helluva lot in common—but we'll always be connected like brother and sister. That helps when the romance comes and goes."

Another megastar marriage beleaguered by the bottle was that of Madonna and Sean Penn. In her 1990 documentary film, *Truth or Dare*, Madonna states that Sean Penn was the one true love of her life, but—as almost everyone predicted—true love was not enough to sustain this volatile pairing. Early in the couple's romance, Madonna gushed, "Sean to me is the perfect American male, and that's all I can say. I'm inspired and shocked by him at the same time." As the liaison progressed, the shocks began to

Valerie Bertinelli has stood by her man, Eddie Van Halen, through the tortures of his alcoholism.

I MET HIM ON A MONDAY

How Rock Couples Met

John Doe and **Exene Cervenka** of the now-defunct X met in a poetry class in Los Angeles.

Bryan Ferry met **Jerry Hall** when he hired her to pose for the cover of Roxy Music's *Siren* album.

Jerry Hall was seated between **Mick Jagger** and **Warren Beatty** at a dinner. Mick was so besotted with Jerry, he went to the phone to arrange for another model to come and distract Beatty, who was also all over her.

Annie Lennox met **Dave Stewart** while she was waiting tables in a Hampstead, England, restaurant.

Tommy Lee met **Heather Locklear** backstage at an REO Speedwagon concert. Lee was smitten on the spot and besieged Locklear's manager's office with calls until the actress gave in.

John Lennon and **Yoko Ono** met when John came to see an exhibition of her art in 1966. Ono didn't recognize Lennon, but he caught her attention when he asked if he could hammer an imaginary nail into a piece called "Hammer a Nail In."

Billy Joel was playing the piano in the lounge of a Caribbean hotel when **Christie Brinkley** walked in. She didn't know who he was, so Joel had to woo her like a mortal.

Madonna met **Sean Penn** when he strolled onto the set of her "Material Girl" video. Madonna says she locked eyes with Penn and "immediately had this fantasy that we were going to meet and fall in love and get married."

John Mellencamp met **Elaine Irwin** when she appeared in one of his videos.

George Michael fell for his makeup artist, **Kathy Leung**.

Ric Ocasek met his wife, **Paulina Porizkova**, when he hired her to appear in the video for the song "Drive."

Backstage at the 1979 American Music Awards, **Prince** slipped **Vanity** a note asking her to bring him into the ladies' room. When she did, Prince asked her if he could try on her jacket.

Keith Richards admired **Patti Hansen**'s "Year of the Lusty Woman" poster so much, he arranged a meeting. When he was ready to propose, Richards told friends, "I'm not going to let that bitch get away."

James Taylor first approached **Carly Simon** (together, above) after one of her Los Angeles performances. Simon says she flirted awkwardly, saying "If you ever want a home-cooked meal..." Taylor interrupted her: "Tonight."

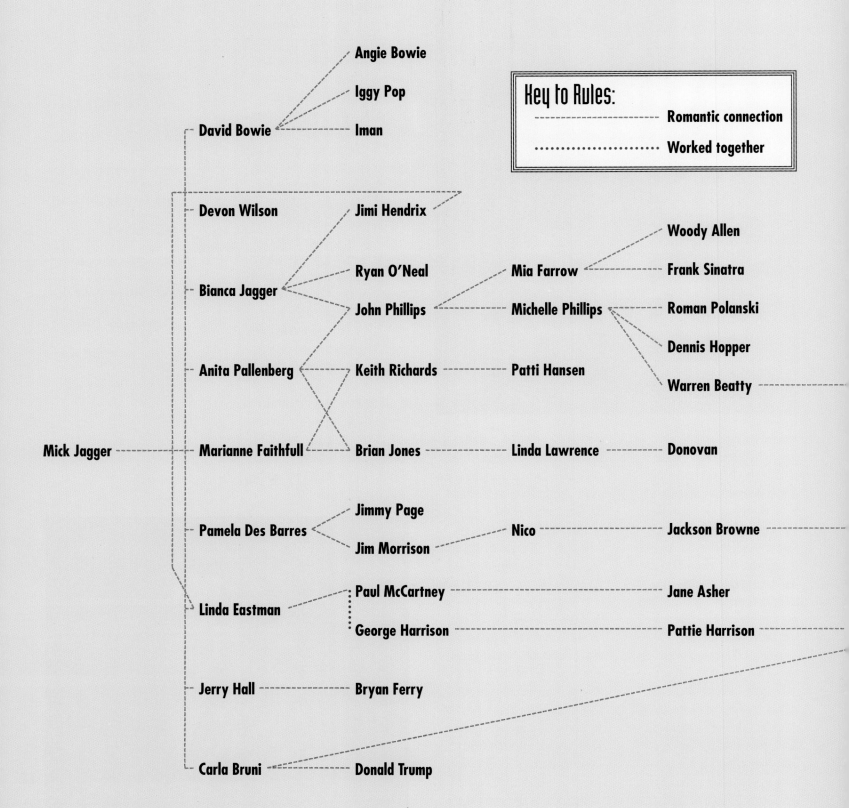

Key to Rules:

-------- Romantic connection

·········· Worked together

Angie Bowie

Iggy Pop

Iman

David Bowie

Devon Wilson   Jimi Hendrix

Woody Allen

Ryan O'Neal   Mia Farrow   Frank Sinatra

Bianca Jagger   Roman Polanski

John Phillips   Michelle Phillips

Dennis Hopper

Anita Pallenberg   Keith Richards   Patti Hansen   Warren Beatty

Mick Jagger   Marianne Faithfull   Brian Jones   Linda Lawrence   Donovan

Jimmy Page

Pamela Des Barres   Nico   Jackson Browne

Jim Morrison

Paul McCartney   Jane Asher

Linda Eastman

George Harrison   Pattie Harrison

Jerry Hall   Bryan Ferry

Carla Bruni   Donald Trump

Julianne Phillips

LOVE IS A BATTLEFIELD

Real and Rumored Rock and Roll Bedmates

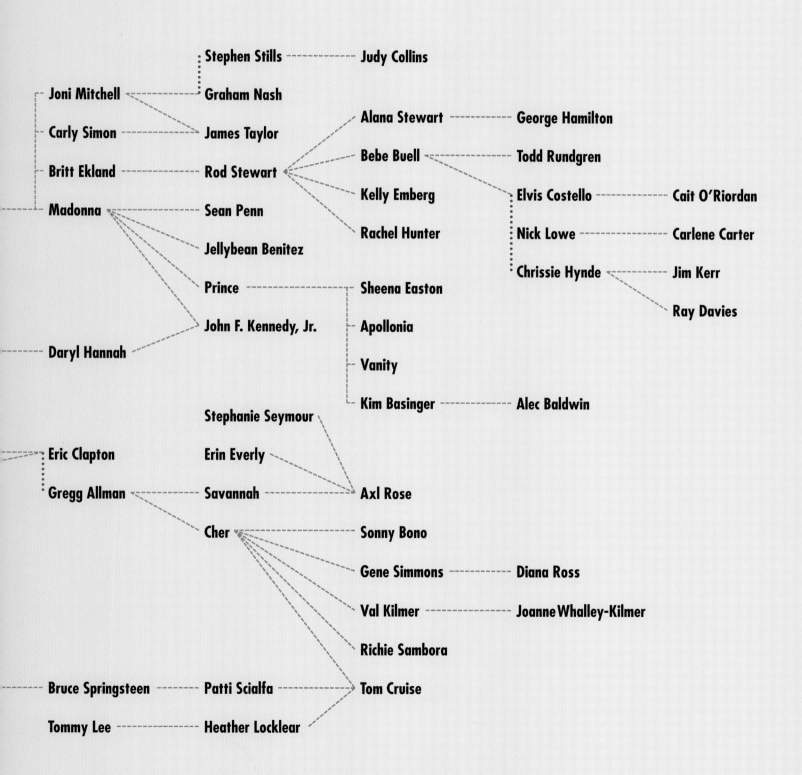

Chapter Five

U Got the Look

FASHION

The Beatles were one of

rock and roll's most

influential trendsetters.

video, rock style has become even more pervasive; MTV and other comparable programming around the world are twenty-four-hour fashion shows.

But the rockers themselves sometimes have mixed feelings about their well-calculated images. Elton John comments, "I get ovations because of the stage clothes I wear. Hopefully, I haven't been trapped by that because, really, there are so many other strings to my bow." (It was, however, John himself who willingly changed his hit tune "Sad Songs" to "Sassons" to make some quick dough from the clothing industry.)

Some musicians are very concerned about being swallowed by their stage persona, and are quick to distinguish

Prince rarely wears this much clothing when performing. In his early days, a typical outfit consisted of black bikini briefs and knee-high black boots.

If the average guy were to put on high heels, tights, and makeup and go down to his neighborhood bar, he might well get beaten up, or at least laughed at. Yet the same people who readily condemn others for their "offbeat" style will scream their lungs out for Kiss, Mick Jagger, or Prince at a rock concert. Rock stars have always been allowed to be fashion renegades, to push the limits of acceptable dress for both men and women, that is, to dress like their fans' exhibitionist fantasies.

For almost half a century now, pop musicians have been fashion trend-setters. From Elvis' sideburns to Beatle boots, from Joni Mitchell's long straight hair to Madonna's jangly jewelry, rockers have set the dress codes for their youthful followers. With the advent of

Rock and Roll REVEALED

between the performer and the person. As songstress Pat Benatar says, "My image is not something I want to do every day. I found this character I wanted to play, and it helped me get over my lack of confidence, my nervousness, my vulnerability. I never considered the character to be a sex symbol. I was just looking for extreme strength and self-assuredness."

"Rock Around the Clock" may have been the first true rock and roll hit, but Bill Haley's Charlie Brown-with-a-guitar look didn't do much to stimulate teen libidos or to revolutionize the fashion world. It wasn't until the pride of Tupelo, Mississippi, came swaggering onto the scene that kids and designers alike took notice.

When Elvis Presley was a child in the southern United States, his family was very poor, so they could afford little in the way of duds besides blue jeans and overalls. High schoolmates remember the teen Elvis favoring loud colors and maverick styles. When Elvis became a pop sensation, though, his flashy fashion sense blossomed. He'd combine red pants, a green jacket, and a pink shirt and socks—anything to make an impression. When he left Mississippi, Elvis never wore jeans again, even when they became chic.

The King and the musicians that followed him helped open the door to colorful diversity in men's clothing. Paul Simon remembers, as a kid, going "all over New York looking for a lavender

Above: Elvis' natural hair color was dark blond. Daughter Lisa Marie, also a natural blonde, prefers life as a bottle brunette, too. Left: Stocky, balding family man Bill Haley was not the sneering rock and roll rebel teenagers were looking for.

U Got the Look FASHION

Right: Brian Jones is credited by some as the pop originator of unisex clothing. Indeed, Jones, though not a full-fledged transvestite, incorporated articles of his girlfriends' clothing into his wardrobe. Below: The 1964 Beatles were a merchandiser's dream; Beatle dolls, wigs, clothes, and more all flourished in the wake of the British Invasion.

shirt like the one [Elvis] wore on one of his albums." The revolution had begun.

Hairstyles, as well as clothing styles, were transfigured by rock and roll. Elvis was mocked for his high pompadour, plastered into shape with Royal Crown pomade. Allegedly, this trademark hairdo was a hybrid of the hairstyle of Elvis' idol, Tony Curtis, and the coif popular among truck drivers in the southern United States during the forties and fifties. The greasy ducktail became a fifties signature, the advent of a new age of "long-hairs."

When the Beatles invaded America in 1964, a lot of media ink was expended on the length of the Fab Four's hair. As the sixties progressed, boys' hair began to creep toward their collars all around the world. Though the Beatles' collarless suits never caught on, every Beatles album cover (and movie) there-

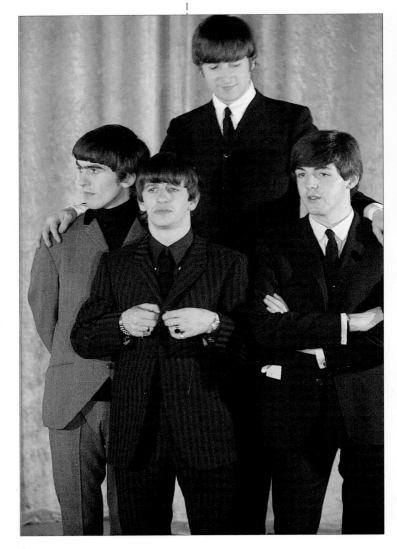

after sent designers to their drawing boards and fans to the stores. (John Lennon's tinted granny glasses are perhaps the most enduring Beatle fashion statement.)

If the Beatles were the lovable moptops of pop rock, the Rolling Stones were their menacing alter ego. The down-and-dirty Stones versus the cuddly Beatles dichotomy was carefully engineered by Stones manager, Andrew Loog Oldham. His creed was, for every Pat Boone there must be an Elvis, for every Beatles there must be a Rolling Stones—thus relegating the Fab Four to lightweight Pat Boone-ism.

Mick Jagger remembers the birth of his outrageous image thusly: "The first time I remember talking about anything that could be remotely connected with image was when I was wearing some kind of layered look, at one of these clubs, and either Brian or Keith said it was too effeminate. I didn't understand why I couldn't be effeminate, or be whatever I wanted, but I hadn't really thought about it."

Brian Jones must have gotten over his fear of extremes in fashion, because he quickly evolved into the Stones' number one dandy. Jones began to layer on silks and scarves, antique

Rock and Roll REVEALED

brooches, beads, and exotic necklaces. On his frequent trips to Morocco, he brought back caftans and Berber jewelry. As writer Al Aronowitz once noted, "Brian was the first heterosexual male to wear costume jewelry."

But Mick Jagger's charisma upstaged even Jones' motley allure. After he starred in the film *Performance*, Jagger started wearing pancake makeup, eyeshadow, and lipstick both on- and offstage. Though his androgynous look has never been adopted by young men en masse, Jagger has always been considered a rock and roll fashion plate.

In the same era, the Stones' counterparts, the Who, were the figureheads for an entire fashion movement. In Great Britain in the mid-sixties, a young hipster was either a mod or a rocker. The rockers adhered to the older Elvis/biker look, while the mods saw themselves as the cutting edge of a slicker, more contemporary style.

Roger Daltrey claims the Who's mod look was engineered by the band's first manager, Pete Meaden. Meaden told the scruffy quartet, "Everybody has long hair. Get yours cut." Daltrey notes, "That was an incredibly dangerous thing to do...to walk in with short hair was taking a very big chance, but it worked.... The mod look was very clean cut, Ivy League, fashion conscious, which was exactly the opposite from the Stones.... Our personalities

Pete Townshend on the mod look: "...you had to have short hair, money enough to buy a real smart suit, good shoes, good shirts; you had to be able to dance like a madman."

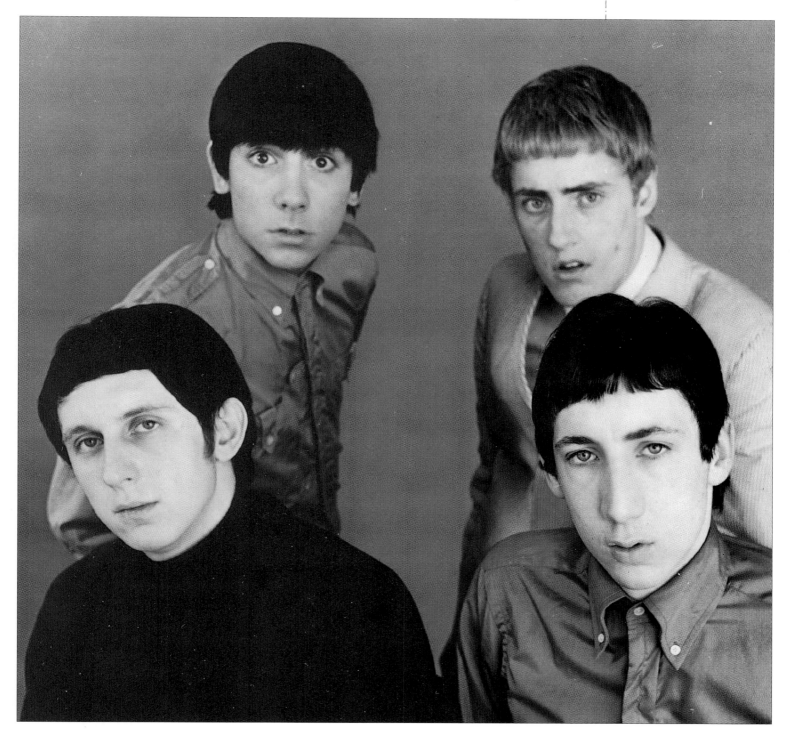

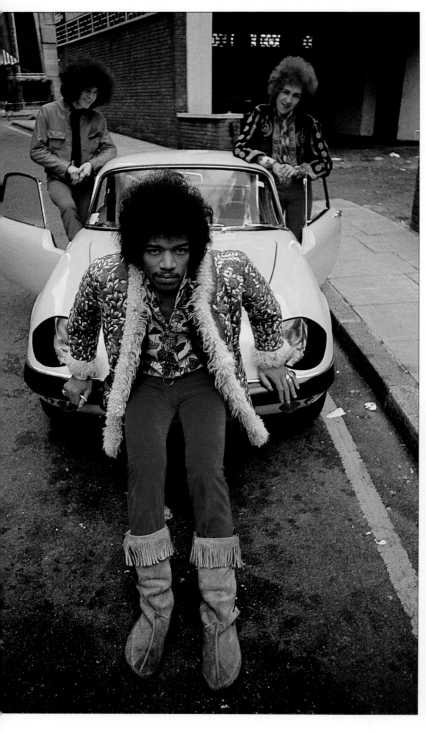

didn't change, we were still a bunch of rotten, dirty-boy rock and rollers, but kids began identifying...it just took off from there."

At the other end of the spectrum from the dapper mod militia was the cosmic gypsy mystique of Jimi Hendrix. As far back as 1964, Hendrix was defying convention with his trailing scarves, outsize Afro, and gold earring. When Hendrix became the toast of London in 1966, Fleet Street dubbed him "the Wild Man of Borneo"; he was certainly like nothing straitlaced England had ever seen. Like everyone else, Jimi was influenced by the Beatles' eighteenth-century-on-LSD Sergeant Pepper look, but he made it his own.

Hendrix's hair seemed to symbolize the freewheeling new age completely on its own. Legions of white British teens tried to tease their hair into the Jimi-do, with feeble results. Jimi himself felt a Samsonlike power to his hair, and was at a loss when he had to cut it for a court appearance. The shy, troubled Hendrix told reporters he would soon grow it back, admitting his Afro was "something to hide behind."

One band whose fans have remained in the sixties' time capsule is the Grateful Dead. Like the band's swirling, country-meets-acid music, the Deadhead wardrobe has remained consistent: jeans, tie-dyed tops, Indian skirts, Birkenstock sandals, and plenty of peace-sign jewelry.

By and large, though, the rest of rock fandom evolved sartorially as the decade changed.

As the seventies began and the mood darkened, the free-flowing, rain-

Above: Jimi Hendrix on his own defiant originality: "Rock is like a young dragon until the Establishment gets hold of it and turns it into a cabaret act with the big voice and the patent leather shoes and patent leather hair." Right: What decade is this?: Grateful Dead fans keep the spirit of the sixties alive in 1987.

Rock and Roll REVEALED

bow-hued look spawned two camps: fringe-and-jeans war-protester restraint and the platform-soled, all-that-glitters glam rock milieu.

The clown prince of the glam rock realm was master of disguise David Bowie. Bowie's otherworldly bent was launched with a childhood fistfight that left the pupil of his left eye permanently paralyzed. By 1972, Bowie's penchant for stage theatrics that included transvestitism made him the perfect founding father of glam rock. Bowie has said he was trying to incorporate elements of theater into the rock milieu, with the singer playing a different role each tour. Bowie's Ziggy Stardust character evolved from mixing Japanese theater with science-fiction imagery. Ziggy was an android from another planet who became a doomed, overhyped pop star. With his brilliant orange spiky hair and ghostly pale skin, Bowie's Ziggy was a haunting specter.

For Bowie's next album, Ziggy mutated into Aladdin Sane, a sort of electric Ziggy with lightning-bolt makeup. When Bowie tired of Aladdin, he set his sights on adapting George Orwell's novel *1984* to rock theater. But Orwell's widow would have none of it, so Bowie grafted Orwellian themes into both his *Diamond Dogs* album and show. Bowie now says that, due to a substantial drug habit, he can barely remember his next character, whom rock writer Timothy White describes as "A blond Aryan dilettante who looked like David Bowie but answered to the sobriquet of the Thin White Duke. Dressed in black but for a white shirt, he stalked a Brechtian set that held nothing but high-tech hardware and sable-colored surfaces, an overhead network of blinding klieg lights lending the ambiance of a Bund rally in an abandoned bunker."

After the Duke's "Station to Station" tour, Bowie cleaned himself up and adopted a lower profile. By the "Serious Moonlight" tour in 1983, he seemed to have settled on a persona he could stick with: David Bowie. In 1990,

A L M O S T C U T M Y H A I R

Distinctive Hairdos and Hair-Don'ts

Annabella (Bow Wow Wow)
B-52's
The Beatles
Elvis
Boy George
Roland Gift
Jimi Hendrix
Michael Jackson
Cyndi Lauper
Annie Lennox
Madonna
Milli Vanilli
Sinéad O'Connor
Slash
Robert Smith
Yazz
ZZ Top

CH-
CH-CH-
CHANGES

The Evolution of
David Bowie

Clockwise from upper left: Bowie as the interplanetary Ziggy Stardust; as Diamond Dog; nineties Bowie, performing with his band Tin Machine; as the Thin White Duke. In the seventies, a pensive Bowie commented, "I believe that rock and roll is dangerous. We...boys with our makeup and funny clothes...I feel that we're only heralding something even darker than ourselves." Opposite: In 1965, David Bowie was still performing under his original name, David Jones. To avoid confusion with the Monkees' Davy Jones, Bowie renamed himself after the hunting knife. Years later, his wife, supermodel Iman, tattooed the knife on her ankle in his honor.

Bowie explained to *Interview* magazine: "I needed to buffer myself with some kind of premeditated identity just to get out there onstage.... I don't think that I need characters anymore. I'm not sure that means I'm cocksure about who I am...but at least I have an understanding that I know myself better."

But Bowie's glam phase had had a solid impact on fashion; for much of the early seventies, followers teetered around in platform shoes, glitter, and iridescently dyed hair. And Bowie was not the only avatar of outrageous fashion in the seventies; he was surrounded, on other stages, by characters just as colorful and diverse as Ziggy and the Duke. From the mohawked, safety-pinned punks to Kiss' year-long Halloween to Stevie Nicks' gossamer witch, there was something for everyone. The punks' self-maiming styles were part and parcel of their protest against bourgeois complacency. Kiss members say their Kabuki makeup gave them a savagely alluring mystique; Kiss singer Gene Simmons claims that groupies often asked him to leave the makeup on during carnal escapades. Says

Simmons, "They wanted the fantasy of being raped by a beast or something." And Stevie Nicks' teenage fans could break out of the schoolgirl doldrums by adopting her ethereal, distinctive chiffon-boots-and-top-hat look.

With the beginning of the eighties, female rock stars had shucked Nicks' fairy-princess styles and settled on a sort of feminized biker image. Chrissie Hynde, Joan Jett, and Pat Benatar wanted to prove that they could rock with the best of them, and "bad girl" black leather became the order of the day.

In an interesting correlation, many male rockers began projecting a softer, retro image. Robert Palmer and Bryan Ferry styled themselves as suited, suave crooners, with gabardine and silk replacing leather and lizard skin. It wasn't long before other bands, such as Duran Duran and Spandau Ballet, and fans, did the same.

Whatever the look, image was now at least as important as the music as the dawn of televised rock video slinked

into its glory days. As Lisa Robinson wrote in *Harper's Bazaar* in 1984, "Now, instant and constant, the rock video images flicker across TV screens 24 hours a day. Hard as some may try, there's no way to escape Annie Lennox's carrot crew cut, Duran Duran's pouty good looks, Boy George's blush-on, Cyndi Lauper's vintage dresses, or Billy Idol's tight leather trousers."

One of the early small-screen stars was not a video-spawned dilettante, but the hardest working man in sequins, Michael Jackson. The single glove, the quasimilitary brocade jacket, and the coyly dangling curl were distinctive focal points. But Michael's androgynous glitter-child image met with criticism from various public figures: television evangelist Jerry Falwell called Jackson a bad role model for youth, Black Muslim leader Louis Farrakhan called the singer's image "sissified" and unwholesome, and even James Brown suggested that the glove might lead to poor penmanship among youngsters. With

Rock and Roll

slings and arrows like these, it's no wonder the Gloved One is so fiercely self-protective.

If David Bowie was the fashion chameleon of the seventies, his eighties incarnation and female counterpart had to be Madonna. In her tenure as Video Goddess, Madonna has tried on just about every pop persona imaginable, from belly-baring boheme to Marilyn Monroe clone to bullet-breasted domi-natrix. The original template—the look that launched a thousand teen wanna-bes—is best remembered in her early videos and the film *Desperately Seeking Susan*. The streetwise urchin Madonna favored black lingerie and midriff tops, accessorized with enough bracelets and necklaces to fill a dime store win-dow. Add a couple of slightly risqué touches—the "BoyToy" belt and a jauntily swinging crucifix—and you've got an instant fashion cult. As a depart-ment store manager said of young fe-male shoppers at the time, "Whatever Madonna was wearing, they'd wear. She's that strong an influence."

The next chapter in the Madonna look was introduced in the video for the song "Material Girl." Madonna had always been fascinated with Marilyn Monroe's sexy yet innocent allure, and elected to impersonate her. Madonna tailored the video to mimic the "Dia-mond's Are a Girl's Best Friend" routine from *Gentlemen Prefer Blondes*. The lat-est Marilyn redux explained the Mater-ial Girl's credo thusly: "You are attracted to men who have material things be-cause that's what pays the rent and buys you furs. That's the security. That lasts longer than emotion."

A perfect role for one who enjoyed toying with boys. Madonna briefly al-lowed her tresses to drift back to au na-turel brown until she metamorphosed into a classic thirties blonde for the 1986 flop film *Shanghai Surprise*. She jumped from the thirties to the fifties for her next look, the pegged pants and Jean Seberg crop featured in the "Papa Don't Preach" video. Madonna

Addicted to clothes: Soul crooner Robert Palmer favors crisp, custom-made suits onstage.

SISTER GOLDENHAIR

Great Bleached Blondes of Rock

David Bowie	Matthew and Gunnar Nelson
Lita Ford	Poison
Kim Gordon (Sonic Youth)	The Police
Debbie Harry	Nick Rhodes (Duran Duran)
Billy Idol	David Lee Roth
Annie Lennox	Dee Snider (Twisted Sister)
Courtney Love	Dave Stewart
Madonna	Rod Stewart
Aimee Mann	Wendy O. Williams
Vince Neil (Mötley Crüe)	Yazz

Above: Eurythmics' early publicity was fueled in part by the rumor that cross-dressing singer Annie Lennox was actually a man. Later stage outfits—such as the red brassiere Lennox sported in a late eighties tour—served to quell this theory. Right: Androgynous Canadian singer k.d. lang has broken through barriers that dictated a feminine look for female torch and country singers. Her stage presence and image has been compared to that of the young Elvis Presley.

explained her mid-decade transition to *Vanity Fair* in 1986: "I wanted to change my clothes. Obviously, if you spend a couple of years wearing lots of layers of clothes and tons of jewelry and it just takes you forever to get dressed and your hair is long and crazy, then you get the urge to take it all off and strip yourself down and cut your hair all off just for a relief."

The new sleek image was perfected for 1987's "Who's That Girl?" tour. The tour's costume designer, Martha Stewart, decided to get rid of all the trademark jewelry and concentrate simply on the star's face and silhouette. But even here, in the tasseled peep-show bustier are the seeds of the next Madonna image: hard-core sex siren. Sadomasochistic and masochistic images fired the singer's "Express Yourself" video, raising eyebrows even in the early nineties, the seen-it-all era. This segued into the gender-bending regalia Jean-Paul Gaultier designed for the "Blonde Ambition"

tour. The male dancers wore brassieres, and the star herself ran the gamut from crotch-grabbing machismo to kitten-without-a-whip modesty. The most famous image from this period is the metallic-coned Amazon in the pink corset with the I-Dream-of-Jeannie hair. Gaultier explains the breastplate design by noting, "A tough outer shell sometimes protects hidden vulnerability."

As is the case with Pat Benatar, Madonna's vulnerability is often obscured by her tough-as-nails image. But no matter what facade she adopts, her electric charisma always shines through. Madonna sees her fashion role as an excavation and redrafting of some of the classic star personas of the century: "Growing up, I admired the kind of beautiful glamorous women—from Brigitte Bardot to Grace Kelly—who [don't] seem to be around anymore. I think it's time for that kind of glamour to come back." Whatever else she may be, Madonna is undeniably glamorous.

Madonna is certainly not the only star to cross fashion's gender lines in recent years. Two mid-eighties sensations—Annie Lennox, formerly of Eurythmics, and Boy George—brought transvestitism into vogue. In the video for Eurythmics' breakthrough hit, "Sweet Dreams (Are Made of This)," Lennox managed to project feminine allure despite her severe tangerine crew cut and tailored man's suit. Later, on a Grammy Awards show, she set the music community a-twitter by appearing as a counterfeit Elvis Presley, sideburns and all. Lennox's former partner, Dave Stewart, accounts for Eurythmics' video-perfect image by observing, "Every band from Presley to Buddy Holly, to the Beatles, to the Kinks has been outlandish. We use clothes not so much as fashion, but to create little surrealist images, stills. Our image is based on clashing, on contrast. We'll take something almost straight and conventional, like a riding coat, then mix it with sun-

SHEENA WAS A MAN

The Gender Benders

Laurie Anderson
David Bowie
Boy George
Michael Jackson
Mick Jagger
Grace Jones
k.d. lang
Annie Lennox
Madonna
Freddie Mercury
New York Dolls
Prince

Rock and Roll REVEALED

glasses, with wild hair and jewelry. It lets us make little statements, underworld statements."

On the other hand, the six-foot (180cm) -tall coquette known as Boy George unabashedly attributed his style choices to pure vanity: "I wear my hair this way because it makes my face look longer, my hat because it makes me look taller, black clothes because they make me look thinner, and makeup because it makes me look prettier."

In the late eighties and early nineties, blatant cross dressing in rock and roll has given way to the ironically macho androgyny of heavy metal. The twist comes at the top: elaborate Farrah Fawcett-esque hairstyles and high-fashion makeup worn with super-stud black leather. Bands like Mötley Crüe, Ratt, Whitesnake, Nelson, and Warrant are equal parts hard rock, sneering stance, and styling mousse.

The epitome of hair-propelled metal stardom is the band Poison. One simply has to ask: would we have been graced with the music of Poison were it not for the tonsorial talents of band member—licensed cosmetologist Rockett? In 1988, Rockett told *Life* magazine how he colors the band's manes: "I'm a walking color mistake myself. Multiple shades of blonde, red here, little traces of purple if you get into the light. A quick lesson in how to ruin your hair."

Bandmate DeVille's bright green streak is a special point of pride. Explains Rockett, "It's throw the black on, then bleach a section and throw the green on." On the road, Rockett has occasionally had to resort to emergency measures like food coloring and Magic

Markers to keep the band's coiffures in working order. On occasion, Rockett has had to defend the band against critics who say Poison is all hair spray and no substance. Says Rockett: "It may be a shallow form of art, but nonetheless it's a form of art."

Perhaps Rockett needs to be reminded that art, like beauty, is in the eye of the beholder.

In the early nineties, the rock world prodded fashion designers in the unlikely direction of "grunge." The Seattle-born look is just what it sounds like: low price, low maintenance, low cleanliness scruff-wear. The centerpiece of grunge is a flannel shirt that looks like it's been through hell. Mike Watt, bassist for Firehose, offers expert advice on classic flannel, "In the flannel world red

is kinda overplayed, but occasionally I'll go for it. Earth tones—brown and green—I can't stand those. Blue is great, and patterns with some white in it—the ultraviolet lights at clubs make it look bad ass." Combine your flannel with faded Levis, t-shirt, and Doc Martens boots—goatee optional—and you're ready to grunge.

The key to effective grunge dressing for both guys and gals is a good, seedy thrift shop. Grunge femmes may opt for retro "granny" dresses (worn with the ubiquitous Doc Martens). Accessories tend to be recycled from sixties' and seventies' fads, such as peace-sign pendants and tie-dye scarves. It would seem that rock fashion, like rock music, is constantly recycling as it re-invents itself for new generations.

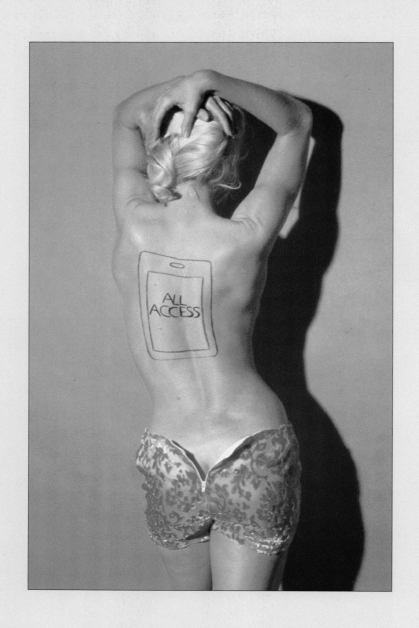

DRESS
YOU UP

The Evolution of Madonna

*T*he many moods of Madonna, clockwise from upper left: A nice Catholic girl—street urchin fresh from Michigan; a boy toy wearing lingerie as outerwear in the mid-eighties; pseudo-Marilyn; Bavarian milkmaid promoting her 1992 photo tome, Sex; sporting the flippy ponytail for the "Blonde Ambition" tour; with a Jean Seberg crop for the "Papa Don't Preach" video. Opposite: Madonna reveals almost all in a publicity shot for her documentary film, Truth or Dare. To see the rest of their heroine, fans had to wait for Sex.

Appendices

Bibliography

Aftel, Mandy. *Death of a Rolling Stone*. New York: Delilah Communications Ltd., 1982.

Arnold, Gina. "Red Hot Chili Peppers; Nirvana; Pearl Jam." *Rolling Stone*, February 20, 1992.

Arrington, Carl, and Roger Wolmuth. "The Chrissie Hynde Story." *People Weekly*, March 23, 1987.

Ash, Jennifer. "Heavy Metal Hair." *Life*, April 1988.

"Baby, They Were Born to Wed." *People Weekly*, June 24, 1991.

Balfour, Victoria. *Rock Wives*. New York: Beech Tree Books, 1986.

Bego, Mark. *Madonna: Blonde Ambition*. New York: Harmony Books, 1992.

Billard, Mary. "Judas Priest: Defendants of the Faith." *Rolling Stone*, September 20, 1990.

Booth, Stanley. "Playboy Interview: Keith Richards." *Playboy*, October 1989.

"Break-Up Is Reported for Jagger and Hall." *The New York Times*, August 1, 1992.

Brown, Craig. "The Rock and Role of Fashion." *Harper's Bazaar*, July 1986.

Chase, Chris. "The Material Girl and How She Grew." *Cosmopolitan*, July 1987.

Choron, Sandra, and Bob Oskam. *Elvis! The Last Word*. New York: Citadel Press, 1991.

Clark, Al. *The Rock Yearbook 1984*. London: Virgin Books, 1983.

Cocks, Jay. "Tunes From the Deep End." *Time*, April 30, 1984.

Cohen, Scott, and Elia Katz. "Brian Wilson." *Interview*, April 1986.

Coleman, Ray. *Clapton!* New York: Warner Books, 1986.

Colman, Stuart. *They Kept on Rockin'*. Poole, Dorset: Blandford Press, 1982.

Cramer, Richard Ben. "The Strange and Mysterious Death of Mrs. Jerry Lee Lewis." *Rolling Stone*, March 1, 1984.

Crosby, David. "The Happy Lazarus of Rock and Roll." *People Weekly*, April 27, 1987.

"Couple Chemistry." *Chatelaine*, October 1986.

Davis, Stephen. *Hammer of the Gods: The Led Zeppelin Saga*. New York: Ballantine Books, 1986.

DeCurtis, Anthony. "Keith Richards." *Rolling Stone*, October 6, 1988.

____. "Henley and Frey." *Rolling Stone*, October 15, 1992.

Des Barres, Pamela. *I'm With the Band*. New York: Jove Books, 1988.

Dougherty, Steve. "After Allegedly Beating His Wife and Shooting Her Car, James Brown May Have to Face the Music." *People Weekly*, April 25, 1988.

____. "Sex and God and Rock and Roll: Prince's Women Try to Explain Their Madcap, Mysterious, Lovesexy Boss." *People Weekly*, November 14, 1988.

____. "Rock's Red Hot Chili Peppers Thrive on Mother's Milk." *People Weekly*, April 16, 1990.

____. "Wilson Phillips: A Trio of Purebred Pop Progeny." *People Weekly*, June 4, 1990.

Draper, Robert. "O Janis." *Texas Monthly*, October 1992.

Dreifus, Claudia. "Still Struggling to Save Her Marriage." *Redbook*, April 1990.

Duffy, Thom, and Larry Flick. "Milli Vanilli Didn't Start the Fire: Vocal Substitution Has a Long History." *Billboard Magazine*, December 8, 1990.

Durkee, Cutler. "Unlike Anyone, Even Himself..." *People Weekly*, September 14, 1987.

Eddy, Chuck. "The Ramones." *Rolling Stone*, September 20, 1990.

"Elton John Won't Go Breaking Estranged Wife Renate's Heart." *People Weekly*, December 5, 1988.

"Eric Clapton and Pattie Boyd Call it Quits After a Baby Boom—His." *People Weekly*, May 23, 1988.

Ewbank, Tim, and Stafford Hildred. *Rod Stewart*. London: Headline Books, 1991.

Fisher, Carrie, and Steven Meisel. "True Confessions, the Rolling Stone Interview With Madonna." *Rolling Stone*, June 13, 1991.

Fleder, Rob. "Black Sabbath: Rock's Demons Never Say Die." *Rolling Stone*, October 19, 1978.

Fleetwood, Mick, with Stephen Devis. *Fleetwood: My Life in Fleetwood Mac*. New York: William Morrow and Company, Inc., 1990.

Flippo, Chet. "Funeral in Memphis." *Rolling Stone*, September 22, 1977.

____. "The Private Years." *Rolling Stone*, October 14, 1982.

Foote, Jennifer. "Not-So-Square Squires; Britain's Rock Rebels Become Country Gents." *Newsweek*, July 2, 1990.

____, and Peter McKillop. "The Many Faces of Cher." *Newsweek*, November 30, 1987.

Frank, Christina. "Why All Women Love Prince." *Gentlemen's Quarterly*, September 1991.

Frankel, David. "John Mayall (Where Are They Now?)." *Rolling Stone*, September 10, 1987.

Freeman, Patricia. "A May-December Wedding Finally Puts a Brake on the Oldest Rolling Stone." *People Weekly*, June 19, 1989.

Fricke, David. "Pete Townshend." *Rolling Stone*, November 5, 1987.

____. "Eric Clapton." *Rolling Stone*, August 25, 1988.

____. "Red Hot Chili Peppers." *Rolling Stone*, June 25, 1992.

____, and Albert Watson. "Lou Reed, the Rolling Stone Interview." *Rolling Stone*, May 4, 1989.

Friend, Lonn M. "1991–2001: Decade of Decadence II." *Billboard Magazine*, September 28, 1991.

Gaines, James R. "The Man Who Shot Lennon." *People Weekly*, February 23, 1987.

Gardner, Ralph, Jr. "On the Road Again." *Cosmopolitan*, July 1992.

Giles, Jeff. "The Milli Vanilli Wars: A Who's Who Guide to the Principal Players." *Rolling Stone*, January 10, 1991.

Gilmore, Mikal. "The Endless Party." *Rolling Stone*, September 4, 1980.

____. "The Allman Brothers." *Rolling Stone*, October 18, 1990.

Rock and Roll REVEALED

Gliatto, Tom. "A Neighbor Says Axl Rose Hit Her With a Wine Bottle, and He Says She's Got a Corkscrew Loose." *People Weekly*, November 19, 1990.

Goldberg, Michael. "The Beach Boy Who Went Overboard." *Rolling Stone*, June 7, 1984.

____. "Mr. Clean: Boy George Straightens Up His Act." *Rolling Stone*, October 8, 1987.

____. "Brian Wilson." *Rolling Stone*, August 11, 1988.

____. "Wrestling With the Devil for the Soul of James Brown." *Rolling Stone*, April 6, 1989.

____. "San Francisco Sound." *Rolling Stone*, August 23, 1990.

Goldman, Albert. "John and Yoko's Troubled Road." *People Weekly*, August 22, 1988.

____. *Sound Bites*. New York: Turtle Bay Books, 1992.

"The Grateful Dead." *Rolling Stone*, August 7, 1980.

Green, Michelle. "Dynasty's Heather Locklear Takes a Motley Mate." *People Weekly*, May 26, 1986.

Green, Penelope. "The Roots of Rock." *The New York Times Magazine*, January 20, 1991.

Griffin, Nancy. "James Taylor, Pop's Rainy Day Man Is Singing a Sunnier Tune." *Life*, October 1985.

Grobel, Lawrence. "Cher." *Architectural Digest*, April 1992.

Grogan, David. "The Days the Music Died." *People Weekly*, April 1, 1991.

Guinness, Desmond, and Bruce Wolf. "A Model Town House: Visiting Jerry Hall at Her Manhattan Residence." *Architectural Digest*, August 1988.

"Half-Hitched." *People Weekly*, May 18, 1992.

Handelman, David. "Is It Live Or..." *Rolling Stone*, September 6, 1990.

"Hanging Out With the L.A. Rockers." *Time*, April 25, 1977.

Henderson, David. *'Scuse Me While I Kiss The Sky*. New York: Bantam Books, 1983.

Henke, James. "Chrissie Hynde Without Tears." *Rolling Stone*, April 26, 1984.

____. "Neil Young." *Rolling Stone*, June 2, 1988.

____. "Jerry Garcia." *Rolling Stone*, October 15, 1992.

Hirshey, Gerri. "Sting." *Rolling Stone*, September 26, 1985.

____. "Michael Jackson." *Rolling Stone*, June 11, 1992.

Hopkins, Jerry, and Danny Sugerman. *No One Here Gets Out Alive*. New York: Warner Books, 1980.

Hotchner, A.E. *Blown Away*. New York: Simon & Schuster, 1990.

"Janis Joplin." *Rolling Stone*, October 29, 1970.

Johnson, Bonnie. "For Bruce and Julianne, No Light at the End of the Tunnel." *People Weekly*, June 27, 1988.

Katz, Gregory. "Inside the Dakota." *Rolling Stone*, January 22, 1981.

Kaufman, Joanne. "Everyone Said It Wouldn't Last...and It Didn't." *People Weekly*, December 14, 1987.

Kessner, Jeffrey. "Stand By Me." *Rolling Stone*, April 6, 1989.

Kunin, James S. "Surprise! It's Splits, Fits and Quits Again for Sean and Madonna." *People Weekly*, January 23, 1989.

Latham, Caroline, and Jeannie Sakol. *"E" Is for Elvis*. New York: Penguin Books, 1990.

Levin, Eric. "Elvis Costello; Rock's Prickliest Songwriter..." *People Weekly*, June 9, 1986.

Lewman, Mark. "How to Buy a Flannel Shirt." *Entertainment Weekly*, March 26, 1993.

Loder, Kurt. "Stardust Memories." *Rolling Stone*, April 23, 1987.

____. "Pretenders." *Rolling Stone*, May 29, 1980.

____. "Bruce Springsteen." *Rolling Stone*, October 15, 1992.

____. "David Bowie." *Rolling Stone*, October 15, 1992.

____. "Keith Richards." *Rolling Stone*, October 15, 1992.

Mansfield, Stephanie. "The Jagger Mystique." *Vogue*, May 1991.

Marsh, Dave. "Keith Moon 1947–1978." *Rolling Stone*, October 19, 1978.

Maynard, Joyce. "Rock Stars and How They Fell." *Mademoiselle*, March 1989.

McKenna, Kristine. "Elvis Costello." *Interview*, April 1986.

____. "Sting." *Rolling Stone*, October 15, 1992.

"Michael Jackson." *People Weekly*, November/December, 1984.

"Michael's Last Tour: Exclusive Pictures From Around the World!" *Ebony*, April 1989.

Neely, Kim. "Berry Faces Drug, Child Abuse Charges." *Rolling Stone*, September 6, 1990.

____. "Osbourne Sued in Two Suicide Cases." *Rolling Stone*, November 15, 1990.

____. "Axl Rose, the Rolling Stone Interview." *Rolling Stone*, April 2, 1992.

____. "Axl Rose." *Rolling Stone*, October 15, 1992.

Nevill, Guy, and Christopher Simon Sykes. "The Model Apartment." *House & Garden*, February 1990.

"No Don Juan Bon Jovi, Jon Marries His High School Sweetheart in a Vegas Chapel." *People Weekly*, May 22, 1989.

Norman, Philip. *Symphony for the Devil*. New York: Linden Press, 1984.

____. "The Rebirth of Elton John." *Rolling Stone*, March 19, 1992.

Norment, Lynn. "Prince's Intriguing Women." *Ebony*, November 1987.

O'Brien, Glenn. "Bowie." *Interview*, May 1990.

O'Dair, Barbara. "X & Drugs & Rock & Roll." *Entertainment Weekly*, August 14, 1992.

Pareles, Jon. "The Trouble With Michael Jackson." *Mademoiselle*, March 1987.

____. "Clothes Make the Musician." *Mademoiselle*, April 1987.

____. "Beauty And The Beat." *Mademoiselle*, June 1987.

____, and Patricia Romanowski. *The Rolling Stone Encyclopedia of Rock and Roll*. New York: Rolling Stone Press, 1983.

Phillips, John, with Jim Jerome. *Papa John*. Garden City, NY: Dolphin Books, 1986.

"Police Blotter." *Rolling Stone*, December 12, 1991.

Pond, Steve. "Belinda Carlisle Comes Clean." *Rolling Stone*, August 28, 1986.

____. "Brian Wilson." *Rolling Stone*, November 5, 1987.

Presley, Priscilla. *Elvis and Me*. New York: G.P. Putnam's Sons, 1985.

____. "We Have Plenty of Time, Little One." *People Weekly*, September 10, 1985.

"Prince's Purple Palace." *Jet*, September 2, 1985.

"Punk Murder." *Newsweek*, October 23, 1978.

"A Punk Way to Die." *Newsweek*, February 12, 1979.

Radovsky, Vicki Jo. "Babes in the Band." *Cosmopolitan*, September 1990.

Raso, Anne. "Heavy Metal: Ozzy Osbourne." *Interview*, April 1986.

Rensin, David. "20 Questions: Gene Simmons." *Playboy*, December 1988.

Ressner, Jeffrey. "Dense Fog May Have Caused Crash." *Rolling Stone*, October 4, 1990.

____. "Freddie Mercury: 1946–1991: Queen Singer Is Rock's First Major AIDS Casualty." *Rolling Stone*, January 9, 1992.

Ritz, David. "The Last Days of Marvin Gaye." *Ebony*, July 1985.

Robinson, Lisa. "Video Stars: Fashion's New Forerunners." *Harper's Bazaar*, August 1984.

____. "The Men of Rock and Roll." *Ladies Home Journal*, February 1986.

____. "Chrissie Hynde." *Interview*, April 1986.

"The Rocker-Model Nexus Meets the Battle of the Sexes as Kelly Emberg Sues Rod Stewart for $35 Million." *People Weekly*, March 11, 1991.

Rogers, Sheila. "A Summer Portfolio." *Rolling Stone*, July 14, 1988.

Russell, Lisa. "A Hot Night in Louisville Puts New Kid Donnie Wahlberg on the Charts With an Arson Rap." *People Weekly*, April 15, 1991.

Saal, Hubert. "Singing Is Better Than Any Dope." *Newsweek*, October 19, 1970.

Sachs, John, and Piers Morgan. *Private Files of the Stars*. London: Angus & Robertson, 1991.

Salvatori, Lou. "Sting: The Rolling Stone Interview." *Rolling Stone*, February 11, 1988.

Sanderson, Laura. "Boy George Comes Clean." *People Weekly*, August 24, 1987.

Schaffner, Nicholas. *Saucerful of Secrets: The Pink Floyd Odyssey*. New York: Bantam Doubleday Dell, 1991.

Schindehette, Susan. "The Perks May Be Great, But Fame Isn't Too Simple for the Fractious Jackson Clan." *People Weekly*, August 8, 1988.

____. "Romancing the Boss." *People Weekly*, October 10, 1988.

____. "After the Loving, Counting the Cost." *People Weekly*, August 7, 1989.

____. "Mick Jagger and Jerry Hall Vow to Spend Their Lives—Not Just the Night—Together, While Bill Wyman Divorces." *People Weekly*, December 10, 1990.

Schneider, Karen S. "Hey Mick Get Offa Her Cloud!" *People Weekly*, August 17, 1992.

Schwartz, Tony. "Bang! It's the Sex Pistols." *Newsweek*, January 16, 1978.

Segell, Michael, "Sid Vicious Accused." *Rolling Stone*, November 30, 1978.

____. "Sid Vicious Dead at 21." *Rolling Stone*, March 8, 1979.

____. "David Lee Roth: Rock's Baddest Boy." *Cosmopolitan*, August 1986.

Shapiro, Harry. "Jimi Hendrix: The Magic and the Mystery." *Rock World*, September 1992.

Shaw, Russell. "'Suicide' Suit Dismissed." *Billboard Magazine*, May 18, 1991.

Smith, Joe. *Off the Record*. New York: Warner Books, 1988.

Snowden, Lynn. "Why Models Love Musicians." *Mademoiselle*, July 1992.

Spitz, Bob. "Raw, Raunchy and Middle-Aged." *The New York Times Magazine*, June 4, 1989.

"A Stilled Voice." *People Weekly*, December 9, 1991.

Tannenbaum, Rob. "The Hard Truth About Guns N' Roses." *Rolling Stone*, November 17, 1988.

____. "Church Assails Heavy Metal." *Rolling Stone*, April 19, 1990.

Van Buskirk, Leslie. "Sean & Madonna: A Year in the Life." *Us*, August 25, 1986.

Wenner, Jann S. "John Lennon." *Rolling Stone*, October 15, 1992.

____. "Pete Townshend." *Rolling Stone*, October 15, 1992.

White, Timothy. *Rock Stars*. New York: Stewart, Tabori & Chang, 1984.

Wyman, Bill. *Stone Alone*. New York: Viking Penguin, 1990.

Zehme, Bill. "Madonna." *Rolling Stone*, March 23, 1989.

Zeller, Mark F. "Cat Stevens." *Rolling Stone*, August 25, 1988.

Song Bibliography

The following song bibliography is organized according to performer. If a song was written by someone other than the performer, the name(s) of the writer(s) immediately follows. Album titles are listed in italics, songs in quotations. Every attempt has been made to give credit where it is due.

America. "Sister Goldenhair," by Gerry Beckley. WB Music Corporation, Los Angeles.

Benatar, Pat. "Love Is a Battlefield," by Pat Benatar and Mike Chapman. Mike Chapman/Chinnicap Publishing, Los Angeles.

Bono, Sonny. "The Beat Goes On." Cotillion Music, Inc./Chris Mara Music, Palm Springs, Calif.

The Boomtown Rats. "I Don't Like Mondays," by Bob Geldof. Intersong USA, Los Angeles.

Bowie, David. "Changes." Jones Music America, New York.

____. "Ziggy Stardust." Jones Music America, New York.

Bow Wow Wow. "I Want Candy," by Richard Gottehrer, Gerald Goldstein, Bertram Berns, and Bob Feldman. Grand Canyon Music, Inc., New York; Web IV Music, Inc., Nashville.

Cale, J. "Cocaine." Audigram Music, Nashville.

Canned Heat. "On the Road Again," by Floyd Jones and Alan Wilson. Frederick Music Company, Chicago; EMI Unart Catalogue, Inc., New York.

Costello, Elvis. "Accidents Will Happen." Plangent Vision Music Ltd., London.

Crosby, Stills, Nash & Young. "Almost Cut My Hair," by David Crosby. Gorilla Music/PRS, London.

The Crystals. "Da Doo Ron Ron," by Phil Spector, Jeff Barry, and Ellie Greenwich. Mother Bertha Music., Inc., Pasadena, Calif.; Trio Music Company, Inc., Los Angeles; ABKCO Music, Inc., New York.

The Cure. "Pictures of You." Fiction Songs, Music Sales Corporation, New York.

The Dixie Cups. "Chapel of Love," by Phil Spector, Jeff Barry, and Ellie Greenwich. Mother Bertha Music., Inc., Pasadena, Calif.; Trio Music Company, Inc., Los Angeles; ABKCO Music, Inc., New York.

The J. Geils Band. "Love Stinks," by Peter Wolf and Seth Justman. PAL-Park Music, Center City Music, Los Angeles.

John, Elton. *Honky Chateau*. Hal Leonard Publishing Corporation, Milwaukee.

The Kinks. "Celluloid Heroes," by Ray Davies. PRS, London.

Madonna. "Dress You Up," by Andrea LaRusso and Margaret Stanziale. Lost in Music, Inc., New York.

____. "Express Yourself," by Stephen Bray. Warner Brothers Music, Inc., Los Angeles.

Newton-John, Olivia. "Physical," by Stephen A. Kipner and Terry Shaddick. EMI April Music, Inc., Terry Shaddick Music, Stephen A. Kipner Music, Los Angeles.

Palmer, Robert. "Addicted to Love." Bungalow Music, Ackee Music, Burbank, Calif.

Prince. "U Got the Look." Controversy Music, Warner Brothers Music Ltd., London.

The Rolling Stones. "When the Whip Comes Down," by Mick Jagger and Keith Richards. Colgems/EMI, Los Angeles.

Springsteen, Bruce. "57 Channels (and Nothing On)." CPP/Belwin, Inc., Miami.

Squeeze. "Black Coffee in Bed," by Chris Difford and Glenn Tilbrook. Illegal Songs, Inc., Hollywood, Calif.

Stewart, Rod. "You're in My Heart." Hal Leonard Publishing Corporation, Milwaukee.

Tone Lôc. "Funky Cold Medina," by M. Young, M. Dike, and M. Ross. Barry White Music and Blue Mountain, Los Angeles.

The Who. "My Generation," by Pete Townshend. Devon Music., Inc., New York; Fabulous Music Ltd. and Westminster Music Ltd., London.

____. "Tommy." Suolubaf Music, New York; ABKCO Music, Inc., New York; Towser Tunes, Inc., New York.

Walsh, Joe. "Life's Been Good." WOW and Flutter Music, Los Angeles.

Wonder, Stevie. "Higher Ground." CPP/Belwin, Inc., Miami.

Index

Photography Credits

AP/WIDE WORLD: 14–15, 27 bottom, 44, 48–49, 55, 68, 70

ARCHIVE PICTURES: 12, 26 (London Daily Express); 36 bottom, 37, 38, 40 top (Miranda Shen); 42 (Bob Scott); 47, 54 right (Philippe Delettre); 57, 60, 64–65, 76, 79 (Frank Edwards/Fotos International); 81 (Tom Gates); 83 top left (Darlene Hammond); 97 left, 98 right, 99, 109 bottom left (Bob Scott/Fotos International)

FPG INTERNATIONAL: 10, 14 left (Peter Borsari); 16 right (Peter Borsari); 46 (Scott Fisher); 48 (Camera Press), 52 (Bob Peterson); 68–69 (J. Sylvester); 94, 98 left, 100 left (Joel Elkins); 103 top right (FPG), 110 (Garry Tausinger)

RON GALELLA LTD: 30, 31, 39 (Belfiglio); 43 left (Kevin Winter); 54 left, 58 (Tammie Arroyo); 59 right (Anthony Savignano); 65, 74 (James Smeal); 77 left (Guastella); 77 right (James Smeal); 83 top right (Kelly Jordan); 83 top center (Albert Ortega); 83 center left, 85 top left, 85 bottom left (James Smeal); 91 top, 103 bottom left, 109 center right (Galella)

GLOBE PHOTOS: 18 left (Alan Grossman); 20 (Ted Kessel); 24 (John Barrett); 27 top (Soren Rud/Camera Press); 41 (Jan Kopec/Camera Press); 43 right, 53, 63 (Philip Gotlop/Camera Press); 75 left (John Barrett); 78 (Steve Finn/Alpha); 80 (Richard Open/Camera Press); 83 center right (John Barrett); 84, 85 top right (Ralph Dominguez); 85 bottom right (Ralph Dominguez); 86 (Corkery/News); 87 (Camera Press); 88 (Mark Ellidge/Camera Press); 96 (Alpha); 103 top left (Wolfgang Heilemann/Camera Press); 105 (Mark Anderson/Camera Press); 106 left (Lisa Rose); 109 top left (Adam Scull); 108 (S. Norris)

LYNN GOLDSMITH, INC: 18 right (Goldsmith); 23 (Jim Graham); 25 (Giovanni Canitano); 32 (Dave Hogan); 35 (Louie Defilippis); 40 left (Jim Britt); 50 (Ron Delany); 51 (Gered Mankowitz); 56 (Dave Hogan); 69 right (Jim Britt); 72 (John Bellissimo); 83 bottom left (R. Corkery); 89 (Dave Hogan); 97 right (Photoplay Archives); 100 right, 101 (Goldsmith); 103 bottom right (John Bellissimo); 104 right (Wayne Williams); 106 right (Steve Jennings); 107 top (Neil Calandra); 109 top right (John Bellissimo); 109 center left, 109 bottom right (Daphne)

RETNA LTD: 16 left (Walter McBride); 17 (Sam Wix); 21 (Adrian Boot); 34 both (George Bodnar); 36 top (Stills); 62 (Stephen Sweet); 67 (Dorothy Low); 75 right (Gary Gershoff); 90 (Arthur D'Amario); 91 right (Steve Granitz); 107 bottom (Alistair Indge)

SYNDICATION INTERNATIONAL: 13, 22, 28 (Dave Hogan), 59 left, 60–61, 66, 82, 102, 104 left